THE LEADER HUMANITY NEEDS

*How to Lead With Heart and Become
a Force for Good in the World*

I0458840

DANIEL TATAJE

TABLE OF CONTENTS

DEDICATION

To Scarlett, my beloved wife, a quiet reflection of Christ's love. Your unwavering devotion, quiet courage, and selfless heart inspire me every day. And to our children—may your lives be shaped by the Love that shaped ours.

This book is also written in loving memory of my father, Felix Edgardo Tataje.

You were my first hero, my quiet teacher, and the truest leader I've ever known.

Through your sacrifice and love, you showed me what it means to lead with heart.

I miss you every day, and everything I do carries a part of you.

I thank God for the gift of your life. I love you, Dad.

INTRODUCTION

We want to be light in the darkness.
—A Dr. Dan One-Liner

H ave you ever wondered exactly which qualities make someone become an empathetic and purposeful leader? It's been over ten years since I asked myself that same question.

When I was younger, I moved from Peru to the United States as an immigrant. But because I had gone to school to become a dentist in another country, I faced a lot of challenges with my licensing. I spent years working as a dental assistant and technician while I managed my unique circumstances. And bureaucracy was just one difficulty I faced—there were plenty of struggles along the way. Eventually, I realized that my gift was leadership and business ownership, and I transitioned from being a team member to leading many. Once I established my growing team, other dentists saw how I led. And some of them wanted to trust me with their own professional legacies—with the dental practices they had spent years or decades building. I was surprised when several different dentists gave me an opportunity to purchase their practices when they retired.

As a result, I grew my dental business from one practice to five. Almost overnight I gained multiple teams under my leadership. That's when I knew that I needed to find a better way to lead. Why? I needed a plan if I was going to be able to influence each team member's life as we quickly scaled. To aid in my efforts back then, I developed what would become the 7 marks of leadership. These concepts have helped me in teaching and becoming the kind of leader who leaves ripples of impact all around them—both at work and at home.

Now, I spend time with other organizations and leaders to help them harness the transformative power of purposeful and selfless leadership as part of my personal mission. And I invite you to join in that mission as a reader of this book. Even if you don't feel like it at the moment, *you* **are the leader humanity needs**.

I want you to know that right now, you are embarking on an amazing journey—one that isn't only for CEOs or business owners. What I want you to see, beautiful and unique reader, is that as a society, we are in desperate need of leaders who are willing to see the gift that each person is while also identifying the skills and talents each person has. This is all so that we can make the lives of those around us infinitely better. As you'll see in this introduction, Jesus, an inspiring leader, helped me realize I want to focus on serving others with my life. If that is something you want also, this book is definitely for you.

My journey has been a humble one. I don't deserve all the gifts God has given me. At my core, I'm a messy human being completely capable of wrecking everything good in my life. And yet, God had blessed my business and trusted me with His unique gifts: the patients who choose my clinics and the team members who work so hard to serve our patients and each other. This motivates me even more to show up as the servant leader they deserve.

Because of the amazing results I saw when I adjusted the way I led in my own organization, I want to help you experience the incredible results that can come from the kind of leadership that focuses on humans first. Those benefits come when we explore and acknowledge our own unique gifts along with the gifts of others.

As a leader, you are valuable whether that's as a parent, an uncle, an aunt, a volunteer, a neighbor, a mentor, a team member of a business organization or a CEO. Leadership is something that every single person can build, whether they're in the professional world or not. And what we really need as a collective society is more servant leaders, especially those who embrace the kind of leadership humanity needs.

Each person you lead is valuable, and they have the power to impact their workplaces, communities, and families, just like you do. Every individual you interact with is a gift, and it is your honor and responsibility as a leader to open that gift to find out how each person you lead can make the world around them a better place with their unique abilities.

In this book, I am going to break down the concepts behind becoming a leader humanity needs while also discussing the 7 marks of leadership that are shaped by the way Jesus led His unstoppable team in the Bible (more on this later). I first came up with this approach when my business was experiencing exponential growth, and I needed to quickly figure out a way to magnify my leadership beyond what I could manage in one-to-one interactions. I couldn't lead and serve a team of 50 people in the same way I had led when I had a team of 5.

When I found myself in that place where my business and team were growing beyond what I had ever imagined, I looked to who I believe is the greatest leader in humanity, Jesus Christ. At that point, my question became: *How did Jesus lead?* The answer I kept coming back to was: *with love.* But that felt like it needed to be expanded if I was going to create a working toolbox of values for myself and my team. After that realization, I went into full discovery mode.

The 7 Marks of Leadership—An Origin Story

Near my home in Wisconsin, I booked a hotel room for an entire week. It was a retreat for myself so that I could get away from everything to focus on developing a toolbox of values that would help others understand how to lead with a humanity-focused approach. I didn't want to be in my normal places as I knew they would bring me normal thoughts. Spending dedicated time on the problem I was trying to solve, away from my comfort zone, was important to me.

Based on the experiences I had in my life and the things I saw Jesus do in the Bible, I spent that week finding, defining, and refining what would become the 7 marks of leadership.

Since we were a dental organization and not a religious one, I also had to put these marks into terms that everyone on my team could understand, even without a Christian background.

Plus I needed to create an order for the concepts I put together so they could build on each other.

These days, with the 7 marks creating a strong foundation for everything in my businesses, Mercy Dental Group has acquired 17 clinics that have since merged into 13 locations. As a group we currently serve over 135 team members (and we continue to grow). Before we get into the foundations we need to build, you need to know what the 7 marks are so you can learn how to use them well.

The 7 marks of leadership are:

- Integrity
- Respect
- Positivity
- Empathy
- Teamwork
- Service
- Humility

These marks are based on the lessons I learned in life and what I experienced through the leadership of Jesus in the Bible. They have helped me create a workplace where people, both patients and team members, feel safe and valued. That is incredibly meaningful to me, and there is tangible evidence of the impact our dental group is having.

We have earned many honors, including being named "Best Place to Work" in *Madison Magazine* multiple times and on the "Top Workplaces" list in *Wisconsin State Journal* in 2022. And in 2021, we were on the Inc. 5000 Fastest-Growing Private

Companies in America list. This is something unheard of for a dental group that is single-family-owned and not backed by investors.

The 7 marks inspire and instruct us to lean into humanity-focused leadership. This guidance helps us treat each person as the gift they are while also encouraging each team member and leader to be a servant, like Jesus was.

It wasn't only at work where I saw the 7 marks change everything though. When I started to use them in my personal life with my family, that's when the people living in my home were completely transformed through empathy and encouragement. And the 7 marks can transform your family and the people you love too.

Now that you know what is inside this book, I want to help you understand who this book was written for.

Who This Book Is For

Here's what I want you to know: This book *isn't* just for leaders in dental medicine.

Leadership isn't only for entrepreneurs or business professionals. Building leadership skills is helpful to anyone who wants to make a difference in the world, including parents, uncles, aunts, friends—any humans who want to see others empowered to make changes in their communities.

That means this book isn't only for people who have official leadership titles. It is for anyone who feels called to lead by God.

Maybe you don't share my faith, and you're wondering if this book will still help you. The answer is yes, these are universal concepts that you can apply to your life.

Anyone can learn about the 7 marks to take positive action. Each chapter will highlight a few stories that shaped my life; the testimonies of others who have used small, persistent actions to change the world; the simplified concepts that guide my leadership systems; the walk-throughs that will help you take action; and the assessments that go with the 7 marks to help you evaluate where you can put in more practice.

Dr. Dan One-Liners

In each chapter of this book, you'll see an opening quote called a Dr. Dan One-Liner. The team members I work with have coined this phrase because of the strong beliefs I share with them over and over again. This is their gentle way of teasing me, and it has become an office joke. But at the same time, they now use these one-liners to encourage each other, which has been both a joy and surprise for me to see. I hope that these one-liners encourage you as you read your way through this book.

What to Expect

In part 1, we will break down each of the 7 marks so that you know exactly how they apply to *your* leadership decisions. Next, in part 2, you'll discover how the 7 marks build on one another to create the positive impact you want to have on everyone around you.

In each chapter, you'll see a summary of points that we worked through and a section called Actions to Take, where you have an opportunity to review the concepts we covered by taking action. Sometimes there will be questions for you to reflect upon and answer. Other times, you'll see assessments that will help you understand the way you currently interact with some of the ideas we'll discuss. The purpose of these sections is to help you better retain what you learn from this book as you apply its lessons to your own life.

Are you ready to become light in the darkness? It is my honor to guide you through the 7 marks as you step into the leader you were created to become.

Blessings,

Daniel Tataje

Chapter 1

MY INTRODUCTION TO HUMANITY-FOCUSED LEADERSHIP

Before you can trust me to lead you on your journey toward more empathetic and purposeful leadership, you need to understand my story so that you know what I'm teaching you really can change lives, just like these concepts first changed my own life.

My First Big Lesson in Leadership

When I first made the decision to stay in my home country of Peru while my family moved to the United States, it was because of money. I chose to focus on my dream of finishing my degree to become a dentist. And while that dream eventually shifted into a vision that came true, and I ended up becoming the leader of over 135 team members and 15 dental brands in the United States, back when I was just a young university student, I didn't know how hard staying in Peru would be. And

I didn't know the amazing lessons that awaited me. That was the beginning of my leadership story.

In Peru, it isn't normal for college students to move out on their own. Staying at home with family gave me comfort and support. And as difficult as dentistry school was during the day, I knew that when I got home at night, my mom would have food made for me. She didn't just cook for me though. My mom, being the caring and loving person she is, would sit with me as I ate and talk me through my day. Each and every day. That anchored me as I worked through the difficulties that dentistry school brought into my path.

Me as an adult with my amazing mother, Rosa, who has taught me so much and sacrificed for me in a loving way

Standing next to my wise and caring father,
Felix Edgardo, who is my hero

Then one day, my parents told me they had decided to move to the United States to help my sister, who had just had her third child. My sister asked them to move, and as retired grandparents who missed my sister's older two girls, they decided that transition made sense for them. My brother had already been living in the US at that point.

Once my parents left, I felt a lot of uncertainty. I didn't know how I would make money so that I could pay to finish school. And I felt more lonely than I ever had in my life.

Because of that loneliness, I spent a lot of time at my then-girlfriend's family home. And because her mother was also caring and loved her daughter, she signed us both up for a ten-week leadership course. My girlfriend's mom told me she hoped that if I went, her daughter would go too. Looking back at the moment now, I laugh when I think about how it wasn't even my choice.

In this class, I learned about leadership dynamics and skills. While my girlfriend didn't finish the class—she had other obligations that were at the same time as the course—I stayed because I thought it was interesting. This was where I met someone who would become a second mother figure for me, my leadership class instructor, Mona.

Mona was a widow who had four children. She had experienced a life of struggles and suffering; before her husband died, he was chronically ill. Years of both his pain and her pain, watching the person she loved go through health-related struggles brought her closer to God. When she spoke, I could see her passion. Mona was also clearly gifted with communication and could say things so clearly.

As a retired teacher, she had a way of helping those in the class understand the wisdom she wanted to share. Her words reached into my soul, and she became one of the most important mentors I would ever have. Mona would say, "With all of the struggles in life, your life is still a gift to the world and you need to share it." She taught us that the words we say and the way we live have power. I'll never forget the sound of her voice when she said, "Your testimony will grab others and drag them into the truth they need to see. So you need to use your life, your stories, and your struggles to impact the lives of the people around you."

I was going through this difficult moment as a young person, trying to find where I belonged in the world. I realized that *I* had the power to create a positive impact in the lives of others. Little me. Having no money. Nothing. I was so inexperienced, but even in that, in my littleness, I could choose to act and to change someone else's life. Why? How? Because I had been gifted with suffering through my lack of resources, like Mona had.

Mona saying hello to the camera with a younger me

I knew that whatever I did with my life, I wanted to live in service to others. I needed to become another positive leader, like Mona. And I wanted to be the kind of leader who thought about the people involved first before I thought about anything else.

That's what I want for you too, amazing reader. It is my goal in this book to help you see that this world needs leaders who understand the responsibility involved in shaping our workplaces, communities, and family homes into more positive places. Each and every person you lead is valuable, far more valuable than the tasks they complete. The people you lead are all gifts with unique abilities. Humanity-focused leadership means that we look at every human as having intrinsic value based on the unique, beautiful, and special creations they are—made in God's image (Genesis 1:27).

As we think about the value of each person, it is also helpful to acknowledge our own value. Do you know how valuable *you* are? Has anyone told you lately that you're amazing? If not, I want you to know that *I* value you. You are a precious gift. And even if you don't feel that way right now, I'm going to prove how much of a gift you are in chapter 2, so keep reading. But first, let's talk about how Jesus fits into my story and this book.

How My Faith Shaped My Leadership Journey

Something else you should know about me is that I am a man of faith. I recognize that I am a messy human loved by a merciful God. That helps me embrace humility, which is actually the single most important trait in a leader. And that leads us back into my story.

With my parents living abroad, Mona continued to mentor me while I finished dental school. After that time, I still felt a longing to be closer to my family, so I moved to the US also. Like I mentioned before, it wasn't smooth sailing as I came with expertise and licensing I had earned in another country. It took 12 years to get to a place where I could finally start growing a practice to follow my dreams (and it didn't happen the way I had imagined it would either). After establishing that first team, that's when I started to get calls from other dentists who wanted to transition their practices to me. It was shocking because I felt like, *I'm just me. I'm an immigrant dentist, not a business person. I don't even have a business degree.* But I jumped in anyway and said to myself, "I *can* do this!" (In the last chapter of this book, you'll see the amazing family member who helped me know for certain that I could.)

At this point, I realized I was suddenly responsible for leading 5 clinics and 40 beautiful, special, unique gifts—the people who God had entrusted me with. This is when I realized I needed to get even more serious about becoming the leader God wanted me to be.

During this new season of leadership, like I mentioned, my business grew ten times overnight. I knew that I could no longer be a daily influence in the lives of all my team members. When we were a team of five total, myself included, I had all my values and was able to motivate all five of us through the vision I could point toward anytime we needed it. But with a larger team, I realized that I needed a clearer road map and system to help everyone understand our identity as a group of clinics. I needed to shape our mission and help each person understand how we were approaching dentistry differently.

It was by God's grace that early on, I realized everyone I was working with needed a common goal to get behind. That was what would unite us as a team, even though there was more than one dental clinic in our growing group. So I came up with what I call a mission identity, which is the description of the purpose we have collectively and is something we could use to describe the identity of our dental group. The mission identity I wanted everyone to pursue was this: to improve the lives of people using our talents, one of which is dentistry.

When we looked at dentistry as a pathway to building relationships with our patients, who grew to trust us with their care, we could create a positive impact in those patients' lives. But in order to do that, we really needed to care about each human being. We needed to know more about them, to ask questions and be interested in their lives, and to open the gift of who each person was. This approach is what I call humanity-focused leadership.

The next question I asked myself was, *How do we interact intentionally with others?* I knew that I needed to give my team members some kind of toolbox that would help them understand how and why we would make every decision. My idea was that this toolbox would be full of the values that had gotten my smaller team to where they were: creating positive impact.

The values needed to be related to business, but they also needed to shape *my* leadership and the leadership of all the people around me. I didn't just want personal development for myself. I was interested in helping each person with their development as a part of our team. Even when people leave our teams, our priority is to have each person leave knowing that they are valuable and unique as a human. This allows them to soar and travel their own paths while creating impact in the lives of others, which is so powerful for them and the people around them.

At this point, I knew that what I needed was bigger than dentistry. Yes, it was important to build relationships with patients, but my question was: *How do I build leadership tools that my team members could use in every part of their lives?* When I look back, this is where the idea of humanity-focused leadership started, and this was when the 7 marks of leadership were born.

Beyond my team, I realized that every person has the potential to be a leader, and that brought me back to when I was 21 and learning from Mona. Then I realized who she was learning from, because like me, Mona had a strong connection to her faith. It inspired me to also think of myself as a mentor, not just to the people I work with, but also to you, wonderful reader.

Now that you know my story, the beginnings of how I became so interested in servant leadership, it's time to introduce you to the 7 marks of leadership in more detail. You and I can both be like Mona to someone else in our lives and keep spreading the wisdom, care, and joy that Mona brought into my life all those years ago.

Part 1

THE 7 MARKS OF LEADERSHIP

Chapter 2

HUMANITY-FOCUSED LEADERSHIP

We're moved by love, not by greed.
—A Dr. Dan One-Liner

In this chapter, I want to help you understand humanity-focused leadership and the foundational principles that shaped the 7 marks I came up with that week in the hotel room. The best place I can think to start is with Jesus Himself.

When I was hidden away in my hotel room/fortress of solitude, the first thing I thought of was Jesus and His relationship with the Father. This led me to thinking about the holiness of Jesus Himself.

You see, Jesus talks about how He was sent into this world to do the will of the Father, not to do Jesus' own will. And I felt that God was entrusting me, Daniel, in all my messiness as a human, with a specific mission as well. When I embraced the fact that I was entrusted with a specific responsibility to make a positive impact in the world, my purpose became even more clear as I looked at the life of Jesus: He had a mission that couldn't be completed by anyone else.

Through lessons from my parents, Mona, and most importantly, Jesus, I learned that we are all uniquely and beautifully created with a specific set of talents. And while each one of us is able to do different tasks, that doesn't mean we are defined solely by those tasks.

Unfortunately, from what I hear in the media and in closed-door meetings with leaders in different industries, many leaders have come to the conclusion that "everyone is replaceable." But I disagree. While any task can be replaced, no *person* can be replaced. We are all gifted with practical and spiritual abilities. The way I use my practical and spiritual abilities is just as irreplaceable as the way you or anyone on your team uses *their* gifts. And because of that, the task of impacting the life of someone else is different for each person.

Based on this journey of thought, I realized that Jesus met us in our humanity by being born as a man himself and entering our human messiness. He ministered to a prostitute, a beggar, and a woman who lived on the fringes of society—because He saw their gifts! Even now, He meets us inside the context of *our* unique abilities and skills. He practiced humanity-focused leadership. And He met the people He ministered to where they were.

Humanity-focused leadership happens when we embrace the unique gift each person is, engaging with the sometimes-messy and beautiful thoughts and feelings each person has that contributes to what humanity is.

I wonder what you would say are your gifts, wonderful reader. How are you already creating impact? How are you already being a light in the darkness? If you've picked up this book, I know you are already taking action to make the world a better place, and the answers to the questions I asked will help your unique mission and value.

When I first had these thoughts, they led me to the conclusion that I needed to know the personal mission I was entrusted with, the thing that made my business unique as an organization, and the unique method I was meant to use as a leader.

As I worked to answer those questions, I turned back to look at the life of Jesus. He was willing to embrace what He knew would be a painful mission. He knew that coming to Earth to be tortured and to die wasn't going to be fun. But He was willing to make those sacrifices. We can even look at the way He came into this world as a humble baby to understand that His whole life shows us His greatness *through His humility*. What does that mean? Keep reading to find out.

How is Jesus' Example Important to Leaders?

Each and every one of us has a mission to follow.

Jesus' humility was one of the most impactful things in His leadership. We can examine it and ask, "How are we called to lead in humility in the places where we have influence?"

Thinking about myself, I strive to be a loving father figure. Not only to my own kids, but to all of the people who are on my team. In fact, when I think about my team members, I call them my kids. And that means assisting the people around me when they face struggles—notice I said "when" and not "if."

As an immigrant to the United States, I have experienced struggles. But these struggles have created some of the most powerful gifts in my life. I always felt that I was not worthy to lead so many people because of my humble beginnings. I didn't feel worthy of the task of writing this book, for example. But I understand that I'm not worthy, and this has helped me approach the way I lead with humility. I know I don't deserve any of this. I still don't know why it's happening to me. But I am sure of this: I am going to do everything I can to respond to the call for me to lead well when it comes to the people who have been entrusted to me.

When I think about humility, I always want to frame it by looking at the example of Jesus. If someone is humble, it doesn't mean they can't be great. I define humility as a low view of one's own importance when compared to others, not a low view of their value or their potential for greatness. Humility is only one of the 7 marks.

As we move through all of the 7 marks, you'll notice that humility is the last mark. Why? The humility of Jesus was the most impactful thing in His leadership. It's last because it is the mark that must be encompassed in every other mark.

For leaders, we have to be open and humble and understand that whatever calling we have, it is beyond ourselves. This is why in business, it is so important to create a mission that will motivate not only ourselves as leaders, but especially the people we lead. And at home with our families, humility encourages us to serve the people in our daily life by treating them with the same importance we give to ourselves. Humility reminds us that the missions we have, both personal and professional, must be prioritized above who we are as individuals. This mission is what helps us keep going when things get difficult.

Before we get into how you know which mission is yours, let's talk about personal, intrinsic value. These concepts are foundational for us as we lead. So let me ask: Do you know how valuable you are? If not, the next exercise will give you an idea.

The Ten Million Dollars Exercise

Imagine that someone says they will give you ten million dollars as a gift today. What would you do if they actually gifted that money to you? There are no strings attached. Would you buy a house for your parents? Would you travel? Where would you go? Would you start a nonprofit to help those facing the same struggles you've worked through in your life?

Give yourself permission to dream. What would that money allow you to do?

First, I want you to think about the lottery. I have a good friend named Luis, who I call Luchon. He plays the lottery each week. One time I asked him why he does it when he knows the odds of winning are so extremely low. He said, "With the few dollars I spent, I get to dream of all the things I would do if I win. That gives me hope."

The lottery as a business is successful because we are willing to buy dreams for a dollar. We're willing to pay for a little bit of happiness and hope.

Now, think back to the ten million dollars. Would you agree that having this amount of money in your life could bring you joy? If yes, I would have to agree. While money can't buy happiness, it can definitely make life easier; having it means there's one less thing for you to worry about.

Now I want you to think about whether you would take the money if there was suddenly one added condition. Imagine that if you took the 10 million dollars, you would die within 24 hours.

Would you still take it? Would it still make you happier?

You might be thinking, *Well, what good is having the money if I don't have my life?*

That's exactly how I think about it. My answer is that I wouldn't take the money.

But once, when I was doing this exercise with a group, I had a woman say, "Yes, I'll take it even if I die." So I asked her, "Why would you take it?," and she said that she knows the money would make lots of people she loved happy. But I pointed out that her family wouldn't be happy with her decision. I told her that even if she didn't value her life as being worth more than ten million dollars, her family did.

She looked at me and nodded, thinking about how her family would respond if they had a choice between the money and still having her in their lives.

You might have answered like that woman, which means you are willing to sacrifice yourself for others. But the value of the money can never even come close to the gift you are for the people you love and who love you.

In short, your life is worth more than ten million dollars. It is worth more than any amount that anyone would give. The help you give others and the dreams you dream with the people around you are worth more than any dollar amount. They would not risk taking the money if it meant you would be gone from their lives. And this question about value leads me to another question about the way we think about our lives.

When we know our lives are so valuable, why do we look so closely at all of the negative things that happen instead of treasuring the value we have? Part of honoring this value is living out each of our unique purposes.

We live in a time where people struggle to find purpose and might feel like this life isn't worth living. This may be from pursuing fake happiness by going after money and material things. But in living our lives for others, we can realize what gives our lives meaning. And that brings us back to Jesus, the very thing He did, living His life for others.

I want you to know that you were loved into life by God. You have intrinsic value. If no one else has told you this before, I want you to know that it's true. You have unique practical and spiritual gifts that God intends for you to use to bless and encourage others. *That is real.* I've seen it over and over again through the people God has brought into my life.

No matter how much you feel or how many others love you or don't love you, please know that you are loved as a beautiful son or daughter of God and that *you* have *infinite potential.* And with that potential in mind, let's talk about how your infinite potential creates and shapes your mission and vision.

The Mission and the Vision

I saw how powerful the 7 marks and humanity-focused leadership could be as I started to build them into my business. I also knew that we needed filters to look through as each team member worked to make the toolbox of these concepts work for them. We all need foundational ideas that will help us focus on the lives of those we want to encourage through humanity-focused leadership.

To help myself and others understand the big picture, I framed two concepts as guiding filters: the mission and the vision.

When we have a clearly defined mission—the overarching goal we want to serve—it gives each person context for how they can use their unique practical and spiritual abilities to work toward the big picture. For each of us, this shapes the specific *way* we choose to serve others.

And when we have a vision—the picture of what we want to see as we help others, not just now but in the future—that helps us look at our mission with new eyes, realizing that this is a long-term ambition. We can work toward each mission, little by little, each day as we build our impact over time to see our collective visions come true.

It is also valuable to know that both the mission and the vision are as important for your individual family as they are for a giant corporation. Like I mentioned before, humanity-focused leadership isn't only for work; it helps at home too.

The reason I'm sharing about the mission and the vision right after you went through the ten million dollar exercise is that once you realize your personal value, you will recognize how the power of individuals coming together with their collective values can transform families, communities, and professional organizations. When we all use the value of each practical and spiritual gift we have as individuals toward a specific goal, the mission can then be executed over time to fulfill the long-term vision. That's when we become unstoppable. And that's what happened inside the organization I serve as a leader. But that isn't what happens in all families, organizations, or dental groups.

The Gift of Mercy Dental Group—A Mission and a Vision

In the world of dentistry, there are a lot of clinics that are named after Dr. So-And-So. But if your mission is to make one person's name great, how can anyone else on the team get on board with that?

When I talk to other dentists, and they ask me what the first thing they can do to inspire their teams is, I ask them to create a mission. And then, I tell them that it needs to be a mission that everyone can get behind. If they have one of those Dr. So-And-So named practices, I encourage them to think about a different name. It's difficult for team members to work hard to promote and grow someone else's name, as opposed to growing a business name they all feel personally connected to.

If you learn to embrace your role as a leader, you will acknowledge that your collective mission is bigger than everyone, including you.

So as a leader, what is the mission you want everyone to get on board with? What is the long-term vision that your mission supports? Defining both will give you what you need so you can share these filters with others when they're struggling and need the motivation of something bigger than themselves to keep serving well. Plus this will give you the answer to: What will inspire *you* to keep going when things feel difficult?

At Mercy Dental Group, our mission is simple. I already shared it with you in the introduction, but I want to show it to you again here, as you think about your mission and your vision as a leader.

Mercy Dental Group's Mission
To transform the lives of people using our talents, one of which is dentistry.

I also have a personal mission, which is:

It is my hope to inspire each and every person I lead—at home and in the office—to embrace the power and value they have to transform someone else's life using their unique talents.

Look at both of those again and think about how they support one another.

It is helpful to notice how the two connect, because when our personal missions and professionals missions are out of alignment, they fight with each other for priority. We want the two types of missions to combine to create a clear path forward for each one of us. And if we don't see a clear connection, not only will we feel a pull in two different directions, our leadership will also pull those who depend on us for guidance in conflicting directions.

When our personal and professional missions align, that is when we will truly see our long-term vision become a reality.

And because it is part of my mission, before we move into the 7 marks of leadership, I want to do an exercise that will help you understand your unique talents and gifts.

How Can We Recognize Which Mission is Ours?

This exercise will guide you as you build your own mission and vision, and I've found that the best way to see how they connect is to write everything out on paper. For that reason, I'm inviting you to grab your journal and pen, or open a notes tab on your phone, to get all of the answers to these questions out where you can see them.

There are two things you can look back on to help you understand the unique mission you've been put on Earth for:

First, look at your path. It's not a coincidence but a gift.

To start, I'll ask you to think about your *personal* mission. Look through these questions and answer them in the context of your personal life.

- What are the things you've been through that have brought you to where you are now?

- What positive things did that path and those journeys produce in your life?

When you look back in retrospect, you have the opportunity to see the gifts you've been equipped with as you've lived your life and your path so far.

Next, think about the answer to the question: "Where am I today?" What you are called to do involves where you are standing right now. Where God has put you.

When you know what you've been gifted along your path and where you are today, you can ask the next helpful question:

- How do I use this path and these talents God and others have given me where I am right now?

Each day, we can move closer to God by using our God-given gifts—ones that God gives us out of His love (because God is literally love). Knowing about His love helps us see the struggles we've had and the lessons we've learned as gifts that can be used to help others feel loved.

You can also ask, "What defines *my* mission?" Answer this based on understanding where God has placed you and the circumstances He has taken you through.

Once we know the answers to the previous questions, we can then ask:

- Where am I headed with this mission? And how can I bring others along?

This is the kind of question that visionaries ask. In the media and in the world of business, we often hear the word "visionary" and think of someone who is almost some mythical creature. But every leader can and must be a visionary in order to create a vision, which we define as a long-term goal we want to see realized in the future. A visionary is simply someone who sees a picture of the future and gets excited about it. All leaders are called to be visionaries, but sometimes we lose sight of creating visions—of what life *could* be. And not just for us, but for everyone around us.

Once you've gone through these questions to determine your personal mission, revisit them to build your professional mission. Then you can evaluate whether you need to make changes to be sure that the two connect and support each other in a clear way.

After you've built both your personal and professional missions and have made sure they complement each other, it's time to build your vision.

Now, answer this:

- What long-term vision do you have for where your professional mission can take you and your team as you use the 7 marks and humanity-focused leadership to encourage your team and serve those around you?

To help you think about *your* vision, I'd love to share a story of how I continue to use our mission as a dental group to help us pursue *our* vision.

Why Do You Do This to Yourself?

One day, I was working with a dental hygienist in one of our offices. I had just announced a new acquisition for our dental group. She said, "You keep growing. Why do you do this to yourself? You're set. Isn't your business big enough?" I thought about her question for a minute, and then answered, "Because I have the responsibility to uphold our mission, which I believe in. This is what we do. The people who are impacted by this acquisition will be in a better position if they are in our group. Why would I choose comfort over the gifts I have that matter to this mission that so many people support? I have to honor these people too. I can sell these businesses and retire—I could spend all day at the beach—but the mission of our dental group is bigger than me. That motivates me. Living life with a purpose is better than sitting at the beach."

The inspiring and passionate Mercy Dental Group team

As a leader, whatever your vision is, I want you to know that you don't have to *try* to accomplish multiple great things in your life. This is where a lot of leaders and visionaries get stuck. What you actually have to do is accomplish a lot of *little* things that add up to *one* great thing.

One of my heroes is St. Teresa of Calcutta. When she felt God's call in her life, she realized her mission was to serve the poorest of the poor. Do you know what she did? She didn't start some huge organization to minister to thousands of poor people. She didn't fundraise. She took 12 nuns from the school she had been working in, and they moved into the slums of Kolkata, India.

Immediately, they noticed that these poor people didn't have access to hospitals, so they worked to create *Nirmal Hriday*, or "Home for the Pure of Heart." This became a hospice home where extremely poor people could be cared for as they died, which allowed them to maintain their dignity.

The nuns took care of those who were dying. They loved them. That was the beginning of what became a huge ministry to the poor.[1] The actions of St. Teresa of Calcutta inspired others as she was dedicated to doing a lot of little things that contributed to one great thing—consistent encouragement and care for the poorest of the poor in Kolkata. And she followed her leader, Jesus, by living out her unique mission.

Since you now know your value (which is far greater than ten million dollars) and you understand how to build a mission

---

1   Melissa Petruzzello, "Missionaries of Charity," *Encyclopædia Britannica*, July 30, 2025, https://www.britannica.com/topic/Missionaries-of-Charity.

others can get behind as you work toward a long-term vision, it's time to begin our look at the 7 marks of leadership. In the next chapter, we'll go over each one so you know what the rest of part 1 in this book is all about. But before that, here's your first summary.

Summary

- When we understand that each person is valuable and loved into creation by God, that will help us approach leadership from a humble perspective, like Jesus did.
- You are worth more than ten million dollars.
- Knowing what your mission is both personally and professionally will give you clarity as a leader.
- Understanding how your personal and professional missions support your long-term vision will help you encourage yourself and others when things feel hard.
- The world needs visionaries, and all leaders should consider themselves visionaries. They help others get excited about a collective mission to create real, lasting impact.
- Being great doesn't mean setting out to accomplish great things. As we saw with the example of St. Teresa of Calcutta, doing small things that align with a clear mission can inspire others and add up to one great thing.

Actions to Take

Think about how you currently approach the way you value others, the way you shape and share your mission, and the way you currently approach leadership. Then answer the following questions.

- Which mentors have shown you how valuable you are in life? What lessons would they want you to pass on to others, based on how they led you?
- Are you looking at your team members as individual, beautiful, and unique gifts? If yes, how? If not, how can you adjust to prioritize this?
- Have you been able to create a mission and a vision that others can get excited about?

Chapter 3

AN INTRODUCTION TO THE 7 MARKS OF LEADERSHIP

A gift none of us deserved was being loved into life by God.
—A Dr. Dan One-Liner

After the self-hosted retreat at the hotel where I came up with the initial 7 marks of leadership, I knew it would take time to refine these ideas. Based on the life of the ultimate leader, Jesus, I continued to develop and test each mark in real time as the team I served grew bigger. Before we get into each one in greater detail, I want to present them in general terms here. Why? Familiarizing yourself with them in this chapter will help you understand how each mark relates to the rest as you read your way through the book.

Let's go through and define each concept together as you start to connect them to create a humanity-focused approach to leadership.

Integrity

The mark of integrity is represented by our desire to hold ourselves to a higher standard, ideally the standards God set for us in His state of being holy. This higher standard leads us into integrity, which I define as the quality of being honest and having strong moral principles. In my opinion, perfect moral uprightness comes directly from a relationship with God. This means that holiness, which I would define as closeness to God, creates a strong foundation for becoming a person of integrity.

Jesus was completely holy during His time here on Earth. Holiness is important because it reminds us that we are working to do the impossible, which is to make a *positive* impact in the world where *evil* exists. Holiness will produce integrity and integrity is necessary to build trust. Trust is key in building relationships and is the ultimate goal of any leader.

Every effective leader needs to be able to build trust to shape their relationships in positive ways so other people can confidently follow them.

For me, behind the scenes, it is my relationship with God that produces integrity as I work toward holiness. I understand that I'm a flawed human being and that I am capable of sin. It is knowing my own potential for doing wrong that helps me stay aware of how important integrity is in every aspect of my life.

That doesn't mean I'm never tempted. Sometimes, in negotiations I feel tempted to lie—to embellish or enhance the truth to make a point. But it's not out of my own greatness that I can resist those temptations. It's through my relationship with God that I am able to maintain integrity in those types of situations.

If I betray God in order to advance something I consider to be part of the mission I believe He has entrusted me with, that hurts my relationship with Him. When I am talking to someone who is entrusting their life's work to me, and my goal is to build a long-term relationship that allows me to be able to look them in the face, I know that I cannot start that relationship with lies. This remains true even if it seems like those lies would help me negotiate better in the short-term.

Even if you don't believe in God, you know there is a difference between good and evil. And making consistent choices to do what is morally correct is essential to lead in both business and personal relationships.

Respect

It is essential for all humanity-focused leaders to treat others with respect; we understand that each person is unique, valuable, and talented.

Since everyone is a beautiful, unique creation of God, we are compelled to love and respect them the way God does. The best way to do this is to recognize what a special gift each person is in our lives—whether that's at home or at work.

When we understand that everyone is beautifully created and loved by God, we can work to spread that knowledge. Not everyone knows that they are loved by God, and not everyone has experienced unconditional love in their lives.

As leaders, it should be our goal to make each person feel valuable. This can be done by doing simple things, such as remembering the names of your team members. And also finding patience for others even when we don't feel patient. Yes, we can all fall into the temptation to lose sight of the value of the people around us, but even then, we can still focus on this important goal to motivate better leadership decisions: to make each person entrusted to us feel loved and respected as the valuable creation they are.

Leaders can also learn how to identify the uniqueness in each person and move them into a position where they will thrive. Professionally, having the unified goal of lifting everyone up will help every member of your team identify what makes each person unique and how that uniqueness plays a role in your organization. At home, you can encourage your family members to further develop the gifts they have by investing your time and resources into those areas you identify as talents.

Positivity

Using the mark of positivity is often contrary to what the world teaches us to focus on, which is the negative. When we assess the positivity in every situation and action, we are free to choose compliments over criticisms.

Positivity is engaged when we actively choose to look at the moments in life that create joy, even when the circumstances around that moment cause intense pain or struggle.

Joy is a noun that describes a feeling of intense happiness, but in the dictionary, joy is also a verb. When we joy in something, we rejoice or celebrate.

Looking for reasons to have joy (or to joy, the verb) will guide us into positivity: We search for reasons to celebrate, even in the midst of difficult circumstances, and that helps us stay positive as we look at our lives. And one way to do this is to observe the gifts we have.

A gift none of us deserved was being loved into life by God.

Positivity and joy are both results of receiving an undeserved gift: When someone gives you something you don't deserve, that gives you joy.

The knowledge that we have received this undeserved gift can only produce joy and happiness in us. We did nothing to earn God's unconditional love. And when we embrace this concept, it will help us understand that everything that comes into our lives—negative or positive—can be shaped to help us, and we are free to share our joy with the rest of the world.

We know that according to the Bible, everything we do, everything that happens to us, whether good or bad, will work for good in our lives when we are working toward God's purposes for us (Romans 8:28).

When we think about how joy gives us an opportunity to engage in positivity, we can realize that even death, the thing that came into the world as a result of sin, is the same thing God used to bring us back to Him through the death of Jesus on the cross.

It is more beneficial to everyone involved when we choose to emphasize the positive qualities of people over criticizing them where they struggle . We should try to help people do better by recognizing the skills that bring them joy. The simple truth that many leaders ignore is: Criticizing people for doing things poorly that they aren't gifted or skilled at won't make them any better.

Empathy

If we treat others the way *they* want to be treated, we are able to really create a positive influence in their lives. But to understand others, first we need to put ourselves in other people's shoes.

We've already established that everyone is a unique gift. Now, I define empathy not as treating others the way *we* want to be treated, but as treating others as *they* want to be treated. Why? Because everyone is unique and they deserve to be treated uniquely.

As a concept, empathy encourages us to look at the circumstances that others go through while considering how it would feel to be in those situations ourselves. Empathy works more deeply than we can imagine when we consider the opportunity to open the gift each person is—by working to understand them better—so that we can unwrap that gift and see what is inside.

I also believe that the concept of mercy is directly tied to empathy. Why? Mercy literally means misery in relationship. Mercy is having your heart close to someone else's misery and suffering in a way that encourages you to want to help them. This means that mercy is active and prompts you to do something about the other person's suffering. Just noticing it isn't enough of a response. Mercy is empathy in action.

Empathy and mercy both involve putting ourselves in the shoes of others to try to imagine their pain. The struggles that others go through create gifts for us by bringing us knowledge and wisdom that can only come out of pain. But we don't always appreciate those gifts. When someone else struggles, suffers, and learns a valuable lesson, they can give us the gift of that same lesson without us having to suffer.

Mercy and empathy are sacrificial. They cost us something when we consider our personal stores of emotional and physical energy. And choosing to act through mercy based on empathy will allow us to truly serve others, especially as leaders.

Teamwork

When we trust each other using the pursuit of holiness to make choices based on the concept of integrity, we have better opportunities to help one another grow and succeed.

That is why trust is the key idea when it comes to teamwork. Earlier we talked about our abilities to identify the uniqueness of each person. Trust in the form of teamwork takes that concept one step further by asking us to move in faith, believing in the abilities of others to do what we need them to do. Successful leadership means helping others find their purposes and talents—the good things they can do and the gifts they are.

We all need each other, which is the beauty of our collective creation, where we live, interact, and become forces for good in each other's lives.

The talents I don't have that someone else possesses are a gift to me when we're on the same team. Leaders have to identify the talents they don't possess and embrace humility to bring people onto their teams who do have those talents. This is where we see how helpful and powerful the concept of humility is to one's leadership. If we look at Jesus' story, we can see that this is what He did: **Jesus built a team.**

Think about how powerful Jesus' team was. With just 12 people, men that would be considered unqualified to work with Jesus through the eyes of the culture of the time, their team was able to overcome the powerful Roman Empire and spread their mission and vision throughout the world.

Teamwork is all about empowering people to work together to accomplish amazing things as part of that collective creation I mentioned. Impossible things, even.

Service

When we serve the people we work with and our families at home, we can aspire to make a difference in the lives of everyone we encounter.

Service leads to happiness. Service means sacrificing for others, and sacrifices prove love is there. When we say "I love you" to someone, what we mean is "I sacrifice for you. I would give my life for you."

Our leadership is more impactful when we become servants for others by sacrificing for and serving them. This is true for the people we work with, who we lead, and for those we all collectively serve as an organization. In our families, we see this most clearly when we look at the way a parent cares for a growing child or in the way a child cares for an aging parent. When we love others in this way, we're sharing happiness with them.

Sharing true love with others is really sharing sacrificial love with them. This is why service is so important in the life of a leader. When I talk about my team, I say, "The people I work for."

If we take time to consider service, we can acknowledge that it's almost unbelievable how much we will give up for the people we love.

At the end of the day, sacrificial love is what gives us fulfillment. We want to build leadership through being servant leaders if we want to see our visions of making the world a more loving place come true. This also means that as we build up leaders in our personal and professional worlds; we inspire them to use their own unique gifts to lead with service-motivated hearts as well.

Humility

When we are humble, patient, and kind, we won't criticize or judge others. We know that we are all unique, talented, and capable of doing anything. Humility is understanding that we each have immense value, but we're not of more importance than anyone else.

A leader who is not humble *cannot* lead in a way that inspires others to follow them.

This means that a leader stands shoulder to shoulder next to every person in their organization. I can't imagine putting myself above any member of my team, because without every person, we cannot complete our collective mission. They are valuable and deserve my respect. Each person's contributions matter, and more importantly, they must matter directly to me as the leader.

One approach I often see is that leaders will try to get team members to follow by saying, "Well, I have this thing they need: money. A paycheck." But that won't inspire anyone to follow a leader or stay with their team long-term.

The best way to lead is to live an inspiring life that causes others to say, "I want to be like that."

Jesus was the ultimate example, and we need to follow the best leader of all time. The central thing that stands out to me about Jesus' way of working with His team is that He saw Himself as a servant to each one of them.

Earlier we talked about how humility is necessary in order to make each of the 7 marks of leadership work well. Without humility, we cannot embrace integrity, respect, empathy, or any of the other marks. And now, we can see clearly why. Humility helps us start from a place of wanting to serve: Knowing our littleness in importance doesn't affect our value or our potential to be great.

Jesus humbled Himself in so many ways during His ministry, and this didn't take away from His value or greatness, especially as a leader.

Summary

- The 7 marks of leadership are a group of qualities that will help shape our leadership to focus on humanity first.

- As concepts for leadership, the 7 marks can be represented by each of the following: integrity, respect, positivity, empathy, teamwork, service, and humility.

- Jesus was the greatest leader, and His leadership was most centered on humility, which empowered Him to sacrifice for and serve others.

Actions to Take

As we think about an effective way the 7 marks of leadership fit together, please take time to reflect on and answer the following questions:

- Of the 7 marks of leadership that were introduced, which one feels the easiest to execute for you?

- Which one feels the hardest?

- What goals can you set for the mark that feels the hardest so that it becomes a bigger part of your leadership style?

- What does being humble mean to you?

Chapter 4

INTEGRITY, HOLINESS, TRUST, AND RELATIONSHIP

Integrity and holiness are two sides of the same coin.
—A Dr. Dan One-Liner

When I was 7 years old and living in my home country of Peru, I had an experience that would go on to define and influence my approach to leadership.

For 5 days in February of 1985, Pope John Paul II visited my country as part of a 12-day apostolic journey. This takes place when an acting Pope travels to Catholic communities or countries around the world. My parents were determined that as a family, we should go see him.

But as a boy who had better things to do, I was irritated that they were making me miss out on playing with my friends and watching my TV shows that day. As you can imagine, the priorities of a 7-year-old boy don't usually include making the journey to see a holy man. Whatever the fuss was, it didn't seem worth the effort to me. I kept saying, "Why do I have to go to this place? I have other things to do."

But all of that changed the moment the Popemobile passed by. Let me explain.

If you aren't Catholic, you might not know what the Popemobile is. It's a white vehicle, usually a small truck with a seat in the back, where the Pope sits during his visits around the world so that people can see him and engage with him.

The Popemobile weaves carefully through the crowds on a planned path, and the Pope waves and looks at the people around him as he goes by. The vehicle drives slowly as he says hello to those who came to meet him in this unique way.

As soon as I saw Pope John Paul II, something happened that I will never forget. Seeing him was one thing, but feeling his presence—that was something completely different. And the feelings I had weren't ones I expected. Even though he was wearing immaculate white vestments, that wasn't what stood out to me. What was really powerful were the loving gestures he made with his hands. And because of the way he looked at me and everyone else around us, even as a boy I felt, *This is the way Jesus would look at me.*

There were so many people, and he was in the Popemobile looking around at everyone and engaging with them with his loving wave. In that moment, I wasn't alone in the admiration I felt for him; I sensed that same emotion coming from everyone in the countless crowd. That's when I realized I was no longer angry about my "important" schedule being interrupted.

Before that moment, though, the intense desire of people wanting to see that holy man had been such a mystery to me.

*I can still remember the way I felt when
I looked at Pope John Paul II*

Seeing him, though, isn't what impacted me. His presence changed me. And over 40 years later, I still remember the love and immense holiness that I felt coming from Pope John Paul II that day. Now as an adult, I know that this holy quality stemmed from the Pope's closeness to God.

I could also sense his humility: Even though I didn't speak directly with him, and even though I was so young, I noticed his humbleness pouring forth through his every look and word. He wasn't there so that we would give *him* personal attention; he was there to put us in touch with God.

When you think about it, John Paul II was a holy man, yes, but he was also the leader of a worldwide organization. He was set apart to take action, his holiness built through being close to God, especially to lead. And through that position of leadership, his goal was to share the love of Christ with the *world*.

The same impact that this man had on 7-year-old me is the same impact you can have with anyone in your life. So how can we create this impact? That day, it became clear to me the one thing that was needed to accomplish such a great feat of leadership: connection to God.

You are set apart to take action and to answer the calling on your life. To understand how, we need to explore holiness and what it means more closely.

What Is Holiness?

The word holiness is often used as a synonym of righteousness: It means choosing to be set apart as morally right and acting with integrity.

When we think about holiness in our failing and sinful human state, it can look and feel impossible. But the word holiness simply means the capacity for being holy. And when you take this to the next level, holiness influences integrity, which speaks to whether we can be trusted.

During His time on Earth, Jesus emphasized prayer and union with the Father every time He was about to enter into each next step of His ministry—whether that was performing a miracle, interacting with someone who needed His love, or suffering on the cross. That was the key to His holiness.

By looking at the Father and Son's relationship, we can see that holiness can only be attained through relationship—through connection. And even though we cannot be 100% holy in our current, sinful state, we can increase our holiness through a closer relationship with God.

Holiness is essential for integrity because your relationship with God compels you to do the right thing, even when no one is watching. When your bond with God is strong, there's only one person you desire to please—Him. When you feel this commitment to God, it will surpass any desire for approval, wealth, or love from the world.

When you truly love someone, you don't want to betray or disappoint them. The same is true when it comes to your relationship with God.

If you don't believe in God, you can still understand how relationships can be improved by thinking of holiness in the context of goodness. When you're connected to someone who you know only wants good for you, that encourages you and influences you to be honest and transparent with them. Often this kind of relationship will influence you to have integrity as a cornerstone for your character.

Holiness as a quality comes from spending time and building a closer relationship with God. That is why not a single moment is wasted when you invest time in deepening your relationship with God.

Time with Him creates a heart in you that will allow you to perform the rest of the 7 marks. In chapter 2, I mentioned that humility is the mark that makes the most impact. What I meant by that is that humility allows us to create the most direct effects on the lives of those around us. But without holiness, we cannot engage the rest of the marks of leadership. For example, when I saw the Pope, I witnessed his holiness and humility in tandem. That was what I felt when he interacted with others and with me.

Our relationship with God is what gives us the foundation we need in order to choose integrity. Without creating a closeness to His holiness through our relationship with Him, we won't be able to resist the temptation to take shortcuts or make selfish decisions when it comes to how we lead.

This is why I say that everything worth doing in life starts with one thing: connection.

The Mark of Integrity

Integrity is one of the most important principles you can embrace in this life. The word itself means choosing to be upright in one's morals: the quality of being honest. Because trust is key in every relationship, you have to work to build this trust, which can only be accomplished through integrity.

When I tell people that integrity is the first of the 7 marks of leadership—and holiness and integrity are two sides of the same coin—I encourage them to think about their closeness to God.

We don't have the power to be morally upright or have integrity on our own. The more we see in this world, the more we notice how imperfect things are. But God, through His holiness, *is* able to perfect us.

If you want to be a person of complete integrity, get to know God, fall in love with Him, and allow that love to transform your decisions. Then, when temptation arises in moments where no one is watching, you will choose what is right—not out of fear—but out of love. This allows you to be a mirror that reflects the light of God. Think about a dirty mirror: It eventually becomes so covered in grime that it loses its ability to reflect light. But when you keep your mirror clean, you can reflect the light of God and become a pure instrument in His hands.

This means that integrity is a result of holiness.

We know that as humans, we all definitely have limitations. Yet, we are set up to achieve the impossible through God. Everything that God asks of us requires being directly connected to Him.

Think about the Ten Commandments. Even if we take one of the most seemingly simple commandments, "Honor your father and your mother" (Exodus 20:12), we can see that this isn't our natural state. As small children, we have to be taught to listen to and honor our parents.

And in general, when we look at all of the commandments throughout the Bible, these things that we are not just called but commanded to do, we often find difficult. And some are downright impossible to do on our own. If we don't have a strong connection with God, we won't be able to do what he has called us to do. And the only thing we are totally capable of on our own, aside from Him, is choosing to sin. Without God it is impossible to avoid sin.

Why does this matter when it comes to leadership? Let's find out.

Closer to God, Closer to Others

I like to say that the fruit of holiness is integrity. Why? Having a closer relationship to God builds integrity. In life, both inside and outside of work, integrity helps us build closer relationships with others.

Looking back, I think this is one reason why others have entrusted me, little me, with the legacies they have created with their dental practices—even when they had better offers from my competitors.

When we are humble enough to know that the way we connect with others cannot be deepened by emphasizing our own individual importance, that is where we start to see real, transformational change in the way our leadership builds up our organizations.

We have so many talented individuals who could do anything impactful with their lives, but they choose to come to our dental group and to stay in our organization. I don't attribute that to *my* greatness but to my ability to build relationships and inspire people to trust me, which is a result of my closeness with God.

In chapter 2, we talked about what it means to find and build a mission. When we look at holiness, it helps if we think about our closeness and relationship with God as the foundational piece for building our other relationships.

As leaders, holiness and integrity will help us to understand that through our mission, the one God gives us, He has entrusted us with something amazing. To really understand how amazing holiness is for providing context in our lives as leaders through our relationships with God and others, let's look at The Gospel of Matthew. Here we learn about how being set apart for action and holiness really connects for leaders.

Investing Talents

In Matthew 25:14-30, we see Jesus give a parable about talents. This most likely isn't the meaning we automatically think of when we see the word "talent."

In this parable, a talent is a word that describes an amount of gold weighing around 34 kilograms or 75 pounds. That's one heavy chunk of gold! Upon writing this, in today's US currency, a talent would be worth around $3.1 million.[2] In Biblical times, a talent would have been worth the equivalent of 20 years' worth of labor.[3]

---

2 Kurt Heckman, "One Talent of Gold Today," *vCalc*, September 23, 2024, https://www.vcalc.com/wiki/vcalc/One-Talent-of-Gold-Today.

3 Dan Kaskubar, "Parable of the Talents Part 1: God's Capital Investment," *Denver Institute for Faith and Work*, October 16, 2025, https://www.denverinstitute.org/parable-of-the-talents-part-1-gods-capital-investment/#:~:text=But%20in%20Jesus'%20time%2C%20a,somewhere%20between%20%24500%2C000%20and%20%241%2C000%2C000.

As Jesus talks to those around Him, He describes a man who is going on a journey, and before the man leaves, he entrusts his servants with different amounts of these giant bricks of gold. To one, he gives five talents; to another, he gives two talents; and to the final servant, he gives one talent. The parable says that the master gives each person the amount that corresponds with the abilities they have.

A long time passes, and finally the master of the house comes back. This is when things get interesting. When he asks what the three servants have done with the talents he gave them, he gets a mixed response.

The first servant said something like, "I took the five you gave me and invested them to double your amount. Now there are ten."

"Wonderful job," the master says. "You were faithful with the few things I gave you, so I'm going to put you in charge of way more."

When the master moves on, the next servant says, "You gave me two talents and I was able to make two more."

"Terrific job, you good and faithful servant," the master says. "Since you did well with the few things I gave you, I will make you a leader in many other things."

But when the master gets to the third servant, the pattern doesn't hold.

When the master asks about the talents, the third servant says, "Well, master, you are a little scary, so I took your talent and buried it in the dirt. Here you go, you have what belongs to you."

The master doesn't like this answer and responds, "You knew I was someone to be feared, but you didn't think I would want a return on what I entrusted you with? You could have even gone to the bank and gotten some interest, but you were lazy."

After he says this, the master has the talent taken from this man and given to the first servant, the one who now has ten talents. The text then says that the person who has gained more will be given even more, but the person who has gained nothing will have whatever he has left taken from him.

As you think about what this parable means in your own life, I want you to know that your first responsibility is to use your own God-given talent—all the things God has put in your life so that you can multiply them.

Next, I want you to think back to what we said about every person: Each one is a precious gift from God, and to understand that gift, we have to open it to realize the unique and beautiful creation they are.

We start with our own talents first, and then move on to all the people God has entrusted us with—those under our leadership.

Now, you might be wondering: How do giant chunks of gold relate to holiness, integrity, and leadership?

God has entrusted us with each person around us, and in each one is profound beauty and many skills and talents (there is that word again).

The master in the story reprimands the third servant for doing nothing with the extremely valuable thing the leader gave him. We have the same responsibility that was given to the servants in this parable.

While we also have a responsibility to others, using our talents begins with us. We need to emphasize that we as leaders must continue to use our gifts and not stay inside our comfort zones. We are compelled to multiply the gifts God has given us first, and in that way, we inspire other people to do the same.

In my own life, I see all the ways God has guided me to this place. This overwhelms me in a good way. I can't help but feel I have the responsibility to respond to these gifts and multiply them. That's why I keep expanding and advancing my mission. The next step is to inspire others to do the same, which is part of using my own talents.

In order to advance and grow the gift that each person is, we want to help them develop their uniqueness, including their skills and talents. (Hopefully I'm doing it for you in this book).

Earlier I said that everything worth doing in life starts with one thing: connection. If we think about the relationship we have with God, the one we can further develop by spending time around Him and encountering His holiness, we know that there is really only one thing required to build a better connection with Him: time.

In the same way, we build better relationships with others as we show them our integrity in action. The connection we need to build with those we lead is also served by investing time with them.

When I think about the amount of time I need to invest focusing on the important relationships I have with others, without God, I can get easily overwhelmed. I have my amazing and gorgeous wife, my 6 beautiful and unique children, and my gifted and wonderful team of over 130 people to think about. They all depend on me in different ways.

This means that when I go to spend time with God, to engage that holiness and integrity, I sometimes don't want to prioritize my connection with Him. Why? Because I think it will save me time to skip over my daily relationship building with God in order to spend it with others I hold dear in my life.

Really though, the less time I have, the more space I need to make for those connections with Him. And here's a story that shows this.

More Adoration, Not Less

In Catholic terms, the word Adoration means a dedicated time of prayer that is spent in the presence of the consecrated Eucharist, which allows Catholics to express, in a personal way, their love and reverence for Jesus Christ. It is a moment of sitting before the Lord and praying in quiet contemplation. This is one way we develop that closeness we want between us and God.

In the writing of St. Teresa of Calcutta, she says that when the nuns would feel exhausted and felt they needed more time or help to keep going, she would encourage them to spend even more time in Adoration. In fact, she says that when they took a break from Adoration, the work they needed to do seemed to double. With extra times of focused Adoration, which seemed like it was stealing minutes from the day that could be spent serving others, they would find the energy and clarity that they needed to be a bigger help to those around them.[4]

Sometimes, we have the tendency in business to want to add more hours to our work days. We think that if we do that, we'll be able to manage better. We might say to ourselves, "I don't have time to pray or to connect with God."

I strongly believe this is why we see so many workaholics.

One thing that will encourage us to set aside time to further develop our relationship with God is to remember that God Himself is the author of time. When we understand this, we realize part of the deep mystery of God that the Bible mentions in Romans 11:33 happens when we notice that our collective hours spent in prayer actually multiply the time we have.

ULTIMATELY, PRAYER IS A TIME *MULTIPLIER.*

Even if you feel like you're busier than ever, you have less time than ever, and you'll never finish all the tasks you have set before you, that's when you need to prioritize prayer and time with God more than ever. Why?

When you do, you'll have more clarity and peace to tackle the list of things you need to do. And you'll also have more time and energy to dedicate yourself to the relationships that

---

4   Sr. Joseph Mary f.t.i., "St. Teresa of Calcutta: A Reflection on Eucharistic Adoration," AirMaria.com | Breathe Freely, August 24, 2017, https://airmaria.com/2017/09/05/st-teresa-of-calcutta-a-reflection-on-eucharistic-adoration/.

God has gifted you with, whether that's at home, at work, or wherever.

And time spent with God also multiplies our integrity. None of us can build organizations that serve others without integrity.

We depend on the trust of the people in our families, our clients and customers, and our team members to inspire and impact them. Without that trust, our abilities to lead will be severely compromised. That's when we might as well be that third servant who hid everything of value in the dirt.

That's why, as we close out this chapter, I want us to take a few moments to think about a concept that is directly related to everything we've touched on so far: stewardship.

Being a Good Steward

In Christianity, the concept of stewardship means that we are responsible for and take action to care about the people and things around us.

Those people God has brought into your life must be part of your personal stewardship.

God entrusting us with others is the real definition of stewardship. Most Christians think about stewardship in terms of money: They bring it to mind when it comes to tithing (giving back time and resources to the Church) and giving to the poor. Yes, those are important things to consider and take action on, but they aren't the only ways we are meant to engage good stewardship.

The most important stewardship is being an administrator of God's riches, and that means taking all of the gifts He has given us into account.

A question I often ask myself to help me engage with stewardship is, *How are you using the talents you have to impact the lives of the people you are entrusted with?*

You see, as a child of God, the first talents to notice are the personal ones. Starting with our own uniqueness, the path before each one of us, and individual skills, we can ask ourselves: What has God provided us with to make the world around us better?

After that, with every person we encounter and lead, we can use those talents—our personal missions and visions—to multiply what we have by helping others use the talents they have been entrusted with as well.

In fact, we can take things a step further when it comes to our stewardship by encouraging others to continue to develop and use their unique skills.

In a sense, we will impact the lives of others by using the talents we have as leaders. Hiding them and using them for ourselves won't create the change we want to see. To make the world a better place, we want to give our gifts to the world. And we need to get to work right now, because this work is going to be hard. We'll touch on this in more detail during part 2, but here's a hint: The resistance we feel to doing good in the world has to do with negative forces that don't want us to make the world better.

I often think of it this way: *When I show my hands to the Lord, does He see the hands of a worker?* I want to show Him my scarred hands because that is my offering: to work hard with the talents He has given me, like Jesus did.

But before we get to the end of this chapter, we need to talk about what stewardship isn't, and I learned this the hard way. Stewardship is not trying to take away the struggles and hard work from those you are entrusted with. Let's find out why.

Standing With Others in Times of Struggle

Caring for someone, being a true steward of the gift they are, does *not* mean taking away their struggles. It actually takes integrity to walk through struggles with people instead of trying to solve them yourself. When you take on the role of trying to solve and provide for all of the other person's needs, you can interfere in *their* relationship with God.

When I was learning how to build a team I could lead well, at first I thought that care meant that I should take on the responsibility of making others happy. I tried to be responsible for everything that went wrong inside each of the practices we had in the dental group.

Soon, though, I realized I was creating a culture of entitlement. My approach was like an invitation to people who wanted to *take* instead of *give*. It created these one-way avenues with some of the people on my teams. I was there to serve them, and so were the other leaders in my organization, but many of those who were receiving that service did not want to return that effort.

That started to affect the culture of the different offices, and I realized the main mistake had been mine.

As a leader, I cannot take away or solve the challenges for those at home or on my work team. But I can give others the tools they need to take on the challenges God has for them.

After some growing pains, I learned that I'm actually here to challenge the people I care about so they have opportunities to become better people while growing and refining their talents. It is my responsibility to help them understand that they have the potential to make the place they're serving better by taking action with their unique gifts in those spaces.

The reason why it is not in the best interest of others for us to try to remove their struggles is because God uses the challenges and suffering we face to draw us closer to Him and to advance His kingdom. It is through our moments of strife that we have the chance to become better educated on what God has planned for us to do as His children.

But that doesn't mean the trials we face will be easy. These struggles cause us each to battle against ourselves, because as leaders, sometimes we might feel tempted to think of ourselves first so that we can avoid discomfort and pain: But this isn't how Jesus leads.

When we look at ourselves first, we can't see the need in the world outside of us. And yes, when we look at the world, we do see a lot of misery and bad stuff. But this is why, as leaders, it will help us to look at the benefits of suffering and to train ourselves in discomfort (which we'll talk about in detail in chapter 11). Self-denial is healthy and part of being close to God, in that holiness can grow when we emulate Jesus in saying, "Yes, I am willing to suffer," like He did on the cross. And even, "I know it will help me to suffer."

If we want to lead like Jesus, it isn't possible without suffering and holiness as goals. Jesus was a good steward of His life in that He completed His purpose. Especially as a leader. That meant He had to focus on others first and be willing to embrace the suffering God had entrusted Him with. Jesus lived for the benefit of not just His team of disciples, but for all of us through the salvation made available at the cross.

Like I mentioned, there is actually a whole chapter about training in discomfort in part 2 of this book, which relates to everything we've talked about in this chapter. But before we get into that, we need to keep building on the 7 marks of leadership.

Summary

- Holiness is the foundation for integrity in action: It grows through time spent with God and guides us away from shortcuts or selfish decisions.
- Integrity flows from holiness and shapes how we lead, both at home and in the workplace.
- God rewards faithful stewardship as shown in the parable of the talents. He entrusts us with more when we invest what we've been given.
- Leadership means modeling integrity in all relationships, building trust, and strengthening teams.

- Prayer is a time multiplier—especially in stress—offering clarity and renewed energy for what matters most.
- Great leaders steward people and talents well, continuously developing their own gifts and helping others grow.
- When we walk with others through their struggles, it helps them grow through it. If we rescue them from the process, that compromises their opportunity for growth.

Actions to Take

For this chapter, the first step I invite you to take is to journal based on the prompts below.

- When you approach holiness in the light of everything I've shared in this chapter (my experience with Pope John Paul II, the parable of the talents Jesus shares, and the way St. Teresa of Calcutta encourages us to pray more when we're experiencing times of struggle), what do you think about holiness and integrity?
- Have holiness and integrity been priorities in your life before?
- If not, how do you plan to change this?
- If holiness and integrity have been priorities for you already, how can you apply what you've read in this chapter to your approach?

The second action I invite you to take is going through this assessment to determine how you think about integrity now that we've discussed what it is and what it does. Please answer yes or no to the following questions.

The Integrity Awareness Assessment

- Do I already spend dedicated time on my relationship with God each day?
- Do I feel that my relationship with God helps me show up as a leader with integrity?
- When I experience stress, do I turn to God directly for encouragement to make righteous decisions?
- On an average day, do I feel connected enough to God to resist the temptations I face?
- When I know no one else is watching, do I still make decisions that support the kind of integrity I want to lead with?

If you answered "yes" to three or more questions, you are well on your way to embracing the first mark of leadership—integrity. If you answered more than two questions with "no," now is the time to make two or three goals based on what you read in this chapter. This will help you better embrace integrity, holiness, and everything that goes along with these helpful concepts.

Chapter 5

RESPECTING THE INNATE VALUE OF OTHERS

Each person we encounter is an entire universe.
—A Dr. Dan One-Liner

Wonderful reader, before we dive into this chapter, I want to share something that is in my heart with you. This part of the book was not written to teach you some strategy that will make you an amazing leader. What you will find here is worth so much more than that. It is my hope that in this part of the book, you will learn how you can literally change the world by giving respect to those around you.

What you read about in this chapter isn't to get you a better bottom line or to teach you how to raise perfect children. Instead, I want to help you understand that the concept of respect can literally change everything for those who exist in your orbit—the people you come into contact with every day.

And not only that, the idea of respect will be just as life-changing for you as it is for those around you.

A lot of times respect is associated with manners. What I mean when I talk about respect is coming to and acting on an understanding that everyone in the universe is a literal gift. You too are a gift, and I definitely want you to know that. But in order for you to truly understand how deep respect can go, I want to help you see that you are not *more* of a gift than anyone else.

When you understand how respect works, it should help you understand how to live your life with purpose. I want you to know that nothing in life is a coincidence; I don't believe that coincidences exist. I know I already mentioned this, but I want to remind you that you were loved into being by God, who created you with a purpose and a mission. If you believe that you were created with a specific mission, a piece of that is learning how to see the people around you in a different light.

And even if you don't have faith in God, you can still acknowledge that there is an uncontrolled aspect of life where each of us is brought unique opportunities that we didn't necessarily seek out (which we'll talk more about in part 2).

There is a strong temptation to use the talents we've been given for selfish reasons, and this can cause us to make decisions that don't serve our visions or missions. For example, are you compromising when it comes to your values because you want to make more money? This kind of compromise will affect not only your ability to respect others but also to respect yourself.

So as we move into this chapter, I want to point toward one of the figures who has given me some of the greatest inspiration in my life, St. Katharine Drexel. Her sole mission was to make a way forward for underserved communities who were not receiving the respect their humanity deserved.

How Katharine Drexel Lead With Respect

Can you imagine being born to a wealthy family, only to end up taking a serious vow of poverty? That's exactly what St. Katharine Drexel felt led to do.

Katharine Drexel, who was born in Philadelphia, Pennsylvania, was the daughter of an extremely wealthy banker in the 1800s, during a time where she was witness to how poor and in need of resources Native Americans were. This grieved her heart and she knew that something had to be done to help them. She was especially motivated to think of their educational needs.

Her father died in 1885, leaving 14 million dollars to charity, and he distributed the rest of his wealth between his daughters. Because of her family's influence, Katharine was able to gain an audience with Pope Leo XIII in 1887, where she begged him to send missionaries to help Native Americans. The Pope surprised her when he said that she herself should become a missionary. Even though she felt skeptical of her own abilities to serve, the encouragement from her local leader, Bishop O'Conner, helped her see that even in her perception of what she lacked, God would minister through her.

After taking up the name "Mother Drexel," Katharine made the decision to give her life and her money to God in service of Native Americans and African Americans.

Drexel went on to found and lead the Sisters of the Blessed Sacrament for Indians and Colored People, primarily located in Cornwells Heights, Pennsylvania, which worked to open Native American schools. In addition, she opened schools for Black students near the border where the different United States switched in identity from being considered the northern states to southern ones. Eventually the Sisters of the Blessed Sacrament founded Xavier University in 1925.

St. Katharine Drexel writing notes

It was because of her leadership in caring for people in underrecognized groups that Katherine was able to bridge gaps in education for those who were generally overlooked. And through her vow of poverty, she used her inheritance from her father to establish Black Catholic schools in over 13 states while establishing 50 missions for Native Americans. She died in 1955 at the age of 96, and she was canonized as the second American-born saint by Pope John Paul II in 2000.

Katherine Drexel respected the people she served by not only showing them care, but by also seeing their value. She provided a way for them to embrace and build that value by receiving the education no one else offered them at that time.

As we further explore the concept of respect, I want to explain what led St. Katharine Drexel to dedicate her life and her wealth to ministering to others who had so many fewer resources than she did. You see, God called her to lead others and herself in this specific mission. He put St. Katharine and her gifts—her talents and resources—to work in the service of others. She was willing to live in poverty because of her mission and love for God. And she led by example in this way. It's not everyone who is called to be poor and give everything they have to others, but in her case, that was her calling.

Your Unique Position

When we look at St. Katharine's life, we can see that she was in a special position. Because of her family's influence, she was able to get an audience with the Pope. Because of her family's wealth, she was able to bring the gift of education to two majorly underserved communities in the Southern United States.

But she is not the only person who was placed in a unique position with a specific calling. God has a particular calling and plan for each one of us. Our calling is directly related to the gifts we have and the mission God has entrusted us with. Even in the midst of whatever struggles you are facing right now, you also have a unique position, and along with that comes a clear purpose.

We are all beautifully created, and we have a special path that is paved one brick at a time using our specific gifts and circumstances and have all been put in place by God. Even the way we look at the world is wildly unique.

Every person is a whole universe.

Each one of us is made up of millions of tiny cells and moments, thoughts and dreams, synapses and responses. Not one of us has had the same experiences or circumstances, even when we're in the same family. For example, while identical twins have the same DNA, they don't have the same experiences because they have unique personalities.

As we walk the path that has been paved for us individually, our particular perspectives on how the world operates are formed.

You are a whole universe, meaning you are a gift to this world. I wish you could look into my eyes and hear my voice as I say this. Even now, just writing this, my eyes fill with tears over how amazing and special you truly are.

As a concept, respect helps us put into action the fact that we recognize how unique and valued each person is: Respect encourages us to treat every person as special. And as we work on understanding respect, we need to bring in its collaborator: compassion. Because if we want to be effective leaders, compassion will help us become more respectful of those around us.

Where the Power of Compassion Comes In

Now you are starting to see why respect matters so much. But respect on its own isn't enough to transform the way we lead and impact those around us. In order to see a broader result for the people around us, we need to pair respect with compassion.

When we acknowledge the struggles of others and validate their feelings, that is when compassion enters the picture.

Compassion works with respect to assist us in imagining what another person may have gone through. Combined, compassion and respect will help us lead better by showing others we appreciate them, even when, and especially when, we disagree. As we explore more in this chapter, you'll see how these different concepts combine for leaders—particularly in my story.

And as God was teaching me this truth about the importance of every person in the history of humanity, I realized I had to understand my own unique position before I could help others do the same.

Counting Every Cent

You already know, amazing reader, that I went to dental school. What you don't know is how many times I felt desperate because I didn't know how I would finish that journey due to tuition costs.

Payment deadlines were constantly running through my mind, pushing me to get creative in the midst of my personal struggles.

In fact, I didn't start out wanting to be a dentist at all. I wanted to be a medical doctor. But after my first year of medical school, I realized that my parents didn't have the resources I needed to continue, and there was no way to make that amount of money myself.

So when I found out that I could go to dental school for one year and then apply for a scholarship based on getting the highest grades in the class, I changed my plans. I asked my father to help me with my first year of dental school, and after that, I won the scholarship.

Things were going smoothly for a while, but then I started needing to purchase expensive dental supplies. And as I started practices with patients (which is when you start seeing patients to practice under thoughtful supervision of professors), I realized my professors weren't going to give me good grades. They all said something along the lines of, "Even today with the extensive experience we have, we wouldn't get perfect scores. So while you're learning, of course you won't have perfect scores either."

I don't think my professors were being malicious. But still, I saw the lack of compassion my professors had for the people they were leading by not setting the standards to something the students could actually achieve. And I wanted to be a force of compassion for my fellow students. I had already been tutoring a few people here and there; when I saw how well the people

I had been tutoring were doing, I was determined to expand that influence based on the compassion I had for my fellow students. Dental school wasn't easy then, and I'm sure it's still difficult now. And the students around me needed to know that someone understood and cared about their struggles. Compassion allowed me to be that person for some of them, and I wanted to provide more of it to others.

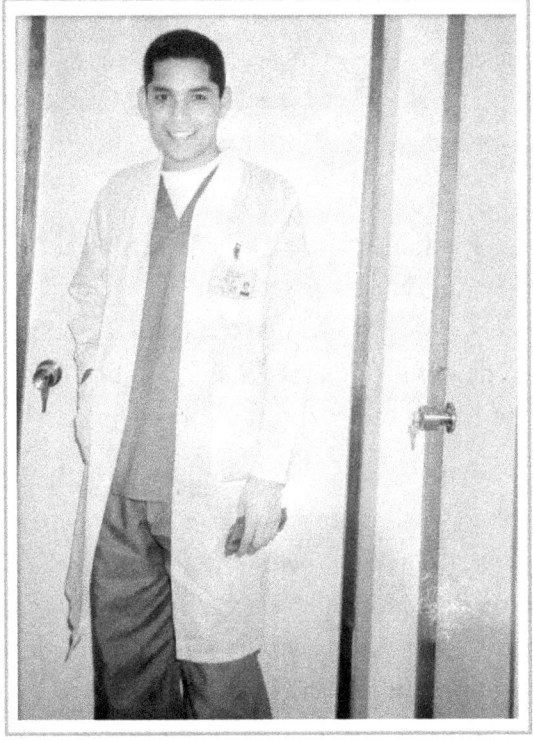

Me as a young dental student

That's when it occurred to me that the tutoring I had been doing on the side to earn some money could help more people if I held group classes. And that expansion would also help me afford my tuition. After that realization, when people came to me for help, I would tell them, "Yes, I would love to tutor you, but you need to get ten other people to join you and the cost for each will be around $20." Not only was I able to buy the supplies that I needed, but the students I helped were doing amazingly well in their classes and they appreciated me. That began my understanding that one of the gifts God had given me was the ability to build businesses.

The tutoring helped me get through to my senior year; however, I still couldn't make what I needed to pay for the final year's tuition. I worried and prayed about it, but I couldn't see a way through.

Then, one day another student asked me if I wanted to be on the student council. I was getting ready to tell him that I wasn't going to be a student for much longer when he mentioned that the student body president got a significant discount on tuition. Suddenly, I saw my only chance to finish school.

When I went to run for the student council, something surprising happened. Because of the number of students I had helped through tutoring, I won by a landslide. Choosing to lead with respect and compassion paved a new road for me going forward. I got the discounted tuition, and since I knew I wouldn't need to be reelected the next year, I made decisions to improve the school without worrying about upsetting the university's administration. That meant I was able to make a significant difference in the lives of others, and that impact felt like part of my unique purpose.

Around the same time, I learned an important lesson that would shape how I treated others for the rest of my life.

Bread and Cruelty

During each break from school every January through March, which were the normal months for summer break in Peru, I visited family in Wisconsin and worked to earn some money on the side to help pay for school. First, I worked the night shift at a bakery, loading bread into trucks all night. It was exhausting and left me sore all over. Second, I worked at a restaurant flipping burgers, which were made of fresh, never frozen beef and had to be made into patties before cooking them.

At this point, I was an adult who didn't speak any English. It felt like a huge disadvantage. I knew that one of my coworkers at the restaurant was saying mean things about me that I couldn't understand. He would say something and point, while he and almost everyone else on the team would laugh.

What I couldn't understand was why he would choose to be so cruel to me. In my heart, I felt a deep anger toward him and I wanted nothing more than to put him in his place. This was when I knew I absolutely had to learn English.

Plus, running back and forth between the bakery and the bread truck showed me that I didn't want to be doing this type of physical work for the rest of my life. Some of my coworkers were well into their fifties and still doing that backbreaking work.

This made me more dedicated than ever to teaching myself to lean into my unique purpose, even though my current position felt bleak at times. It was through these struggles that I came to know that I am an entire universe.

As I looked at how far I had come, I knew that choosing kindness and helping others succeed in dental school is what had been propelling me forward. So when I looked at the situation at the burger place, I didn't want to be like the mean coworker who laughed at my expense just because I didn't understand English.

Looking back, I often ask myself, *Daniel, when you recognize that you have these scars, what does that mean for the people around you? Are those scars part of your uniqueness? Do they shape your special gifts? How do the depth of these scars make you an entire universe?*

You see, dear reader, I realized that this coworker didn't see me as a gift. He didn't care about getting to know me, which would open up my uniqueness to find out what kinds of gifts I could bring into his life and the lives of those around us. But I had the opportunity to learn from his mistake—and now, so do you.

Looking Through the Lens of My Scars

Now when I think about the way I lead, I look at everything through the lens of the scars I have—a universe's worth of experience. In order to get to where I am now, I had to go through some seriously uncomfortable moments. Whether it was the physical pain in my back caused by loading bread from the bakery into the truck or the emotional pain I experienced while my coworker was cruel to me because I was from a different culture and spoke a different language. Those moments shape how I lead today.

By looking at the struggles we've had, we can realize how much more of a gift those around us are. Now when I see people doing physical labor, I am so thankful for them and their related gifts. And when I have someone on my team who I know is doing work that is physically demanding, I think about how I would have wanted to be treated and led by my supervisor in the bakery.

I also work extremely hard to make sure that cruelty isn't acceptable in our teams. I never want one of our team members to feel the way I did working with that coworker at the burger place.

You can also look through the lens of your scars. Would you say that as a leader, it is your responsibility to set the tone for everyone around you? To show them how you love everyone as you imitate God, so that they see the value in respecting others?

You can't love something you don't know.

When I think about my coworker, it doesn't surprise me that he didn't respect or value the gift that I am; he never put in any effort to get to know me, which was his mistake.

That same unconditional love that you receive from God, it's not something that comes naturally to any of us. But we can each work to understand it and then show it to those who are gifts in our lives.

I don't regret the way that coworker treated me because it taught me a valuable lesson: Every person I encounter is worthy of respect and love, and they are worth getting to know.

The Mark of Respect

Once I grappled with my own innate value, I started to realize how powerful it was to recognize and respect that same innate value in others.

In my story, you can see the many struggles I faced. I needed more financial resources to recognize my dream. Other people didn't see or acknowledge my innate value, which made it more important to be clear on the gifts my personal uniqueness presented.

Before I could help anyone else, I needed to make sure I was in a good position myself. Think about it this way: When you have a lit candle, you can share that flame to light the candles of others. But if your candle is out, you can't possibly share that light. This goes back to one of my Dr. Dan One-Liners: We want to be light in the darkness.

In order to embrace my own value, to light my own candle first, I needed to take the time to clearly see the way God showed me love and respect, so that I could do the same for others. I needed to move past the way my coworker at the burger joint made me *feel* to embrace the truth about what God made me *to be*.

This totally reframed the way I looked at the people around me and then worked to help them. At this point, I knew that the respect I had wanted from people who dismissed me was an important part of how I would lead. And when I hid away in my hotel room to research the way Jesus led, I could see this as one of the main ways He worked with those He came into contact with.

Jesus was a respecter of persons, but not necessarily the people society would have expected him to respect. He reached out to those who would otherwise be considered on the fringe of society. He refused to give into the ruling class when they demanded He defend Himself against the Jewish council called the Sanhedrin.

You see, Jesus didn't automatically show respect to the people who society said He should respect. He invited a tax collector to join His team (Matthew 9:9-13). He welcomed an encounter with a woman who was so sick, she had been a total outcast of society (Luke 8:43-48). Jesus looked at the hearts of people, and He interacted with them accordingly—no matter what position they did or didn't hold.

And when I understood this, I discovered that the gifts and situations that God gives us shape the way we can impact the world.

For example, when I say, "It's a pleasure to meet you," I truly believe it. In fact I believe you are the only you in the history of humanity, and that is an honor to be cherished. And while I don't necessarily explain that to every person I meet, I need to think about it and act in a way that reflects that belief.

This is the true meaning of respect: to understand that the other person you're with is important and amazing. And when they give you some of their time, which they can never get more of, that should be treated with care and admiration.

We are naturally pretty good at respecting others and their time when we're dealing with celebrities or people with money or power. But we often need help to realize and remember that these people of influence aren't more important than any other amazing person. When we think about how we act toward someone we know is famous, there should be no difference from the respect we show everyone in general.

If someone is meeting with you, they are choosing to spend time with you when they could be anywhere else in the world. They could be with their families or doing something they love instead. But they are investing their time, the only resource we can't make more of, with you..

If you are giving me your time, you are giving me your life. That deserves the utmost respect.

What About Me?

On the other hand, you might be wondering, *What about me, Daniel? I'm giving them my time as well. And I'm valuable too, right?*

I totally understand why you might want to ask that question. At the same time, that question can be dangerous in that it has the potential to brush away any respect you're trying to have for the other person. Relationships are about giving, yes, but when someone is giving you their time, you're also receiving. You are being enriched by this other person's life. And any person can enrich your life, regardless of their financial situation or social standing.

But you as a person definitely do factor into this equation of respect and innate value.

When you define your personal worth, your amazing uniqueness, by how loved or accepted you are by others—in a sense—you don't think you are enough.

It will help you to light your own candle first. You have to value yourself. Respect is a two-way street. It might feel like your focus needs to be completely on the other person you're interacting with, but that's not true. You cannot respect others when you don't first understand that you are also a gift.

Loving yourself means there's a line between honoring others by having the heart of a servant and putting yourself in a position to be abused. You are valuable too, and you won't be able to love others well if you can't love yourself first by avoiding relationships that have the potential to be extremely damaging to you.

This is where we might be tempted to choose people-pleasing behaviors over behaviors based on respect. Please don't do something someone else wants you to if it compromises your values. You are worthy of love, so worthy. And if others don't choose to respect you, you still need to respect yourself.

In the story about flipping burgers and the cruelty of my coworker, I learned from his behavior. I knew that reaching out to him or trying to build a relationship with him wasn't worth my time. What I needed to do was stay away from him whenever I could. But I also needed to find a way not to hate the guy. I didn't want anger for him settling into my heart.

So I chose to look at him with compassion based on his innate value, and now that's a lesson I use every day. I would say that lesson was well worth the struggles I faced with this man.

This is why we need to pair compassion with respect when it comes to how we lead. When we can choose to act with compassion by taking into consideration that not everyone has the supportive people they need around them—those who teach them to make choices that are motivated by integrity—we will be able to look at the world through the lens of our scars.

And by combining respect with compassion, we can lead in a way that honors the uniqueness of every person we have the privilege to influence.

Imagining Their Story

One of the best ways to help us understand how to respect those who might not value our innate uniqueness as much as we value theirs is to remember that we don't know their full story. This is also where compassion and seeking to understand the other person's circumstances comes in.

To guard my heart against bitterness when it came to my burger place coworker, I reminded myself that someone else had probably done something to him that caused him to choose cruelty. And also, I couldn't do anything to make him happy.

He, like all of us, was a result of his experiences. And there are many out there who lived through difficult circumstances.

But from a leadership standpoint, we can still choose to see others with compassion while refusing to tolerate disrespect from them.

Once I had a patient come in and the first thing out of her mouth was, "I don't even know why I'm here. I hate dentists because the only thing you want is money. But my granddaughter said to talk to you, so here I am."

I was able to acknowledge mentally that she most likely had previously met with an abusive dentist, but I didn't want to focus on that with her. Through imagining her story, I was able to build context for her feelings without being personally offended. Next, it was my goal to move our appointment forward. I knew her expectations were low, so it was my goal to exceed them. At the same time, I wanted to do what was right to help her.

Compassion and Respecting Others and Ourselves

We can be compassionate with others while still respecting ourselves. We do not need to let someone abuse us; we are also valuable. Choosing compassion doesn't mean we have to do the will of others to compromise our own values: We are as worthy of love and respect as anyone else.

This woman eventually became one of our happiest patients, and she still loves coming into one of our offices to this day. Why? Because I imagined her story and that helped me understand where she was coming from. I showed her compassion without compromising my values or allowing her to make me feel like I'm not also worthy of respect. And then, we bonded.

When I onboard new team members, I run the orientation personally. I want to show each person how much I respect them, because I want them to be able to show that respect to our patients. I want them to feel that it's a deep honor for me that they choose to come in for the orientation on their day off. It is my responsibility to make them feel valued and respected.

I share with each person how amazing and special they are. They know by the tone of my voice, my posture, and my facial expression that I mean everything I'm saying. And this is why it is so important to get in a physical room with them. That is also when I share my personal mission and how I want to support them as they work to make our company mission and vision come true. And often, when I do this training, I get tears in my eyes. That's how precious these people are to me.

When I work with my staff, I see myself as the motivator for each person to act and to find out what their talents are so that they can use them.

My respect and compassionate words help each of them to know how thankful I am that they are doing the things in the office I cannot do. As a leader, I can't always be there to interact with and touch the lives of the patients directly, but affecting the lives of our patients is my goal and mission—and also the collective goal of our entire organization. Through the smiles and healing touches of my staff, they help me with that mission by serving those who come through the doors of our different offices.

Sometimes, with a full schedule, we can get in a rush. That's when I remind our team that some of our patients are lonely. That one of us might be the only person the patient talks to that day, and something as little as a smile or a conversation can be huge to them.

Just because we have a full schedule doesn't mean we can't meet patients with compassion. This realization can be one of the greatest struggles we face in this life.

God created us to be loved, and that's why we crave love from others.

It is in my heart to share with you that you are a gift. You are worthy of respect. And I thank you for who you are, not what you do. Your ability to do your unique job in your special calling will reach the hearts of other people as you lead with respect and compassion as well.

As you lead your team members, you can build respect within them by showing respect and by teaching them directly how to show it to others.

In the next chapter, we are going to build on the marks you've learned so far by exploring how positivity can shape the way we think and lead.

Summary

- Embracing respect will help you, and those around you, live to promote everyone in finding their unique purpose. Every person is a gift to be opened.
- You can't love or respect what you don't know.

- St. Katharine Drexel saw the innate value of others, and she dedicated her whole life to their cause.

- When God brings struggles into our lives, we can use the scars that are left to help us look at others with compassion.

- Respect means that you understand each person is amazing, important, and should be treated as such, with admiration and care.

- In order to respect and love others, we must first love and respect ourselves.

- When we choose to imagine the stories of others and treat them with compassion, it will help us to work through our anger and still keep our individual value.

- When we show others respect, we are teaching them how to show that same respect to the people around them.

Actions to Take

Spend some time journaling through the following prompts to expand your thoughts about respect and compassion.

- Do I value myself and respect myself? If not, what are some ways I can show myself compassion as I work to embrace the entire universe that God made me?

- When I think about my past, is there anyone who I feel was disrespectful to me? Can imagining the causes of that behavior in their life help me shed compassion on the situation for myself?

- Do I feel like I ever agree with people who are asking me to compromise my calling or my mission? If yes, what steps can I take to distance myself from those people?

(Think back to my coworker at the restaurant. While I worked through the disrespect he showed me, did I continue to try to get close to him?)

Chapter 6

THOUGHTS OF POSITIVITY AND FEELINGS OF JOY

The small action of igniting a candle casts light much further than you think.
—A Dr. Dan One-Liner

I don't know about you, but for me, it took years of deliberate thinking to set my brain's autoresponses to positive instead of negative.

I thought that embracing self-pity was a normal part of the human experience, and that kind of thinking got me into all kinds of trouble. At some point I realized that I could either spread negativity or positivity to those around me, both at home and at work, even when I say seemingly small things or take what I thought were unnoticeable actions.

This is the way I explain positivity to my team, and even more importantly, to my children:

When you ignite a candle, you think that it is a small movement. But your action, as small as it seems, can inspire other people to ignite their candles as well. That's when all of a sudden you are all casting a huge amount of light together, made out of a million candles.

You don't know how far your little action of igniting one candle can spread. Think about being in a stadium of darkness. What happens when the first person ignites their light and others follow? All of a sudden, the darkness is gone.

In the first chapter of this book, I shared a one-liner with you that says, "We want to be light in the darkness." When leaders embrace the dynamic changes that positivity can create, this is how we choose to be that light.

But how often are we taught about the true benefits of leading our families and teams by choosing to act based on positivity? We live in a world full of negativity and criticism. In the stories of our lives, we see how many of the things we experience could be considered negative: Sometimes we lack resources; sometimes we experience language or cultural barriers to the spaces we seek entrance into; sometimes we try so hard, but in response to our effort, we experience nothing but struggle.

But if we only look at the obstacles we face as negative experiences, we cannot see how these same circumstances can give us immense gifts that shape who we will become.

When we switch our filters to viewing things in a positive light, that's when we can truly see how the struggles we face give us opportunities that couldn't come any other way.

Changing Your Filter—A Dot Thought Experiment

While there isn't a conclusive source for this story, I think it beautifully illustrates the concept of positivity. It involves a black dot on a white piece of paper.

This almost urban legend[5] retelling starts with a group of college students waiting to hear that day's lesson from their professor.

When the man steps into the classroom, he tells the students that they will be having a surprise test. The anxiety in the room suddenly rises as everyone tries to figure out the subject of the test.

As the professor hands out the exams, the students look up at him, a wordless question on each of their faces. All that the test contains is a small black dot on each full sheet of white paper.

"Now, I want everyone to write about what they see on the test," the professor says.

At first, no one in the room knows how to respond to the professor's prompt. But as time passes, each student begins writing—each one hoping they understood the point of the surprise exam—until all of them are finished.

Once the professor collects all of the tests, he tells the students that they don't need to feel nervous, as he has no intention of actually grading the exams. Then he proceeds to read each and every answer out loud.

---

5   Donna Kersey, "The Black Dot," *God's Other Ways,* November 30, 2020, https://www.godsotherways.com/stories/2020/3/25/do-the-next-thing-4baw5-8faz4-8858t-9sdzk-pajgn-arlfb.

Finally, after he finishes reading the last answer, he says, "Almost every answer you gave is about the tiny black dot on the piece of paper. What many of you neglected to see was how much paper there was around the black dot. In comparison, the dot itself is a tiny fraction of what is actually there on the page. This is a lesson I want you to take with you for the rest of your lives: When we only focus on the negative, which in this case is symbolized by the dot, we miss out on all of the amazing things that are also happening in our lives, which is symbolized by the expansive white space on the paper."

The students had to be trained not to focus on the dot so that they could see the page full of potential. And that is what we can train ourselves to do as well.

So let me ask you, wonderful reader: If you had been in that classroom, would you have focused on the black dot or the white space of potential? Take a moment and consider how you would have responded before and how you would respond now—knowing what the professor shared with the class.

Now, let's dive deeper into the mark of positivity to learn what it can do for us as leaders.

The Mark of Positivity

None of us are born angry.

It is through the experiences we have in the world that we are trained to default to negativity, which can in turn fuel anger (and other feelings that can sidetrack our leadership goals like fear or anxiety). But when we look to the example that Jesus set for us in His specific style of leadership, there are clues that help us understand how to reset our default thinking patterns based on the way He interacted with those around him.

As we look at the stories in The New Testament, we see that over and over again, Jesus meets the people who have been torn down by society by encouraging them in a truthful way. Jesus meets with the woman at the well who shows up in The Gospel of John (4:1-11), and Jesus speaks hope into her life—even though everyone else from her village has been avoiding her because of her multiple marriages and her current relationship where she's living with a man she *isn't* married to.

Next, we see the example of Jesus and Peter. During Jesus' condemnation from the Sanhedrin and Pontious Pilate, Peter denies knowing Jesus three times. When Jesus ministers to Peter after this happens, Jesus confronts the denials, but gives Peter encouragement by reminding Peter of his loving relationship with Jesus (John 21:15-23).

Jesus used encouraging words even in negative circumstances to build up those around Him, and we can do the same.

When we look at the way that positivity can enhance our lives, it helps us to notice that when people are not affirmed with praise as they grow up, they will first need to experience someone else noticing positive things about them to be able to shift their own filters.

This is where the mark of positivity comes into the life of every leader.

Many of us have heard the same resounding and unfortunate advice: The way to lead is to point out everything the person is doing wrong.

This is why in the professional world, there are personal improvement plans (PIPs). Anyone who gets one of these plans knows the truth—they are one step away from being fired.

Can you imagine having a PIP hanging over your head, and at the same time, feeling free to unlock and develop your talents? It doesn't seem like those two things go together, and yet, this is how many professional spaces attempt to get team members to level-up their skills.

The problem with current leadership approaches, both at work and at home, is that we often forget to compliment those around us—we neglect to point out the positive things other people are doing. At the same time, when we see problems, our first instincts aren't to bring solutions into the room where we plan to discuss these issues. We feel like the first step is to point out who created the problem.

I have found that when I teach from a place of encouragement, the person I'm working with is much more likely to excel than if I teach from a place of criticism.

And when I enter the room with a list of possible solutions, the positivity in that room expands exponentially.

Maybe you can relate. Think about the teachers and leaders who have helped you the most in your life. Did they approach you from a place of wanting to build you up or a place of wanting to tear you down? Did they come with solutions or only complaints?

As leaders, we simply cannot forget to highlight the positive actions that our team members are taking. And when leading those in our families and communities, the same concept is true.

We often have a mentality that anything positive that someone does is part of their job or their responsibilities, so they don't need praise. I cannot tell you how many times I have heard other professionals say that if they praise their teams, the people on those teams will become lazy. But in my experience, that assumption couldn't be further from the truth.

If someone is doing an excellent job at something, that's wonderful, but even then, compliments will build them up and encourage them to keep going. And the compliments don't have to be meticulously planned grand gestures. Instead, they can be simple words of encouragement.

It is helpful to remember that by staying positive about the areas where we lack skill, and instead of being critical about those missing talents, we can count on those around us to fill in those gaps. For me, this result is another source of joy. When I notice my personal limitations, I am acknowledging that I need the help of others who are all unique and amazing gifts in and of themselves.

People who work with me learn how to compliment others about the small things they do to build more supportive professional communities. This could mean complimenting something as seemingly small as a coworker changing their hair or getting a new outfit.

When we model this type of behavior for our team members, we're teaching them to encourage each other. This is a way to help those under our leadership give and receive love. Interactions based on this encouragement bring so much joy to my heart as their leader. This practice is also why respect and compassion are such powerful concepts when we think about how to lead. When we praise others and compliment them through the lenses of respect and compassion, this builds positivity in the work environment.

This is how we create a workplace that is contagious with joy.

Spreading Joy and Second Chances

One of the biggest values that comes out when we focus on positivity is that we can spread joy to the people around us.

By now, you already know that I believe people flourish through compliments instead of criticism.

But I want you to understand that you can bring pure joy into someone else's life by seeing the positive in them.

A successful leader is one who sees virtues first. This doesn't mean we ignore the vices or failures of that person, but we do come into our relationship with each person in an attitude that focuses on solutions. Even though there is a problem to solve, we don't assume the person who is struggling *is* the problem. Instead, we choose to see their virtues—their character, their talents, and their efforts—first. That way, we can team up with the amazing things they are already bringing to our team as we approach whatever problem there is.

My approach is simple. I tell my team, "Let's solve this problem together. I want to help you out."

This means that we look at the mistake or difficulty together, and we come up with a solution that isn't based on criticizing or disciplining the team member who made that mistake. When we team up to create a solution, we're solving the problem together.

You already know that one person is an entire universe. And when we look at them through the lenses of encouragement, positivity, and joy, this means we resist the temptation to compare them to anyone else. (This is something we explore more in chapter 14.)

At one point in my business, we approached hiring a new team member without the normal vetting order we would otherwise use. This person made it to their final interview with me before we ended up doing a background check.

Once we saw what had happened in the person's past, the entire team wanted to discuss if it still made sense to onboard them. I said I wanted to talk to this person about what had happened in their life to make sure we weren't reducing them to the list of mistakes that had been populated on their report.

When we met, this person explained everything about their past situation with sincere regret and an attitude of wanting to do better in the future.

I informed the team that I felt strongly that we needed to give this person a second chance. We needed to love them with positivity and joy into who they were meant to become.

Years later, this person is such a joyous addition to our group and is in a position that could only be entrusted to someone with the utmost integrity. This person became a huge gift to everyone on our team.

Imagine, wonderful reader, what would have happened to this amazing and unique creation if we hadn't brought them into a positive work environment where they could grow their confidence and skills.

Failure presents each one of us with a unique opportunity that will allow us to grow.

This is why if you have the power to encourage someone, you should use it. We need people in our lives to grow, and they need us to grow too. We can share the lens of: I need you to teach me something today, and I need to teach you something today.

When we realize and act on these principles, based on noticing the whole white page in positivity instead of only focusing on the small, black dot, this is where joy comes in. And joy has the power to encourage each one of us to take real action to make the world a better place.

Unfortunately, though, not all leaders choose to encourage their team members with positivity and joy. And we're going to see such a story, one that I've shared part of before.

The Sad Closing to a Chapter in My Life

In the last chapter, I told you all about the coworker who made fun of me for not speaking or understanding English well. What I didn't tell you was that I actually saw this same man many years later when I took my family to the restaurant to show them the place where I had worked in the past.

I can't tell you how many times I had thought about what a reunion would be like if I ever saw him again. Now that I could speak English fluently, I would finally have an opportunity to confront him about what he had said about me to the staff all those years before.

But seeing him again didn't go the way I had thought it would.

After a few minutes of showing my family around the restaurant and pointing to the kitchen where I had flipped so many burgers, I suddenly felt a familiar presence.

When I looked up, I couldn't believe what I saw.

That coworker who had made my life so miserable, the one who had gossiped about me to everyone in our workplace, was there. In the same restaurant. Doing the same tasks decades later.

All of the images that had danced through my head before that moment, thoughts about making him face me and the way he had treated me as someone less valuable, faded away.

What I felt, instead of pride in my accomplishments, was a deep sense of sadness for that coworker's continued situation.

How is it possible that he spent all those years doing the same thing? I thought. What had gone wrong in his life? Why hadn't any of the leaders in his life encouraged him through positivity so that he could do and become more? Sure, we had made different choices, but I didn't think he would still be there wiping down tables and taking orders.

In that moment, I was flooded with emotions I hadn't really ever felt before colliding into each other. I was so thankful for my positive outlook and the joy it had brought into my life. And I saw that the damage he had done through gossiping about me to others had possibly hurt him because of his negative filter. At the same time, I realized his negativity had helped me learn to be resilient in the face of struggles.

Along the way, from flipping burgers to leading a dental group with over 130 team members, I learned that even the person who has hurt you the most in your life has made you better.

I wish that my coworker had learned that lesson as well. I wish someone had helped him see that he is an entire universe and was worthy of love so that he could learn to share joy and positivity with others.

I believe gossip has the power to destroy, but kind, positive words have the potential to create life. Which force are you going to use to better lead those around you?

In the next chapter, we're going to talk about a mark that helps all of the other 6 marks fit together in a more effective way: empathy. Because when we understand how to place ourselves in the shoes of others, that's when we can really learn what kind of respect, positivity, and integrity they need to be modeled for them to become the gift they were always meant to be.

Summary

- In life, even small actions can encourage positivity in others, like igniting a candle so that others can be inspired and do the same.

- When we are conscious of the things happening around us and for us, even the biggest struggles can feel positive.

- In the dot thought experiment, the students mostly commented on the small black dot, not the entire white page. We can remind our brains to focus on positivity by being open to seeing all that is there, not only the small things that we struggle with.

- Jesus led by example, using positivity to build up those around them, even when they had made mistakes.

- Positivity means focusing on encouragement over criticism.

- When we encourage those who are doing things well, that doesn't mean they will become lazy or complacent. In fact, they are more likely to find joy from compliments and perform even better.

- If we judge people based only on their mistakes, we miss their potential. We miss the gifts they are.

- Gossip has the potential to destroy, but positivity and joy can take us out of struggles to help us build a more encouraging future.

Actions to Take

Journaling to See the Positive in Struggles

Take time to journal about the ideas of positivity and joy using the following prompts:

- Who has been the most hurtful person to you in your life?
- What opportunities did you have to learn from those experiences?
- How can you frame what you learned in a positive light, even though you disagree with that person's choices?

The Negative to Positive Shift Assessment

Now take the following mini assessment to help your brain understand what it feels like to shift from negative and criticizing thoughts to those that are positive and encouraging. Write down how you could change the thought from negative to positive.

- The people in my life who have hurt me most have damaged me in irreversible ways.
- Failure is telling me to quit and that I'm unworthy of unconditional love.
- When I look at myself in the mirror, I wonder where all of my potential went.
- Struggles in life make me feel less capable of living out my personal mission.

Next, think through the following questions as you shift them from negativity to positivity:

How can you embrace joy when you think about the way you're reframing these thoughts? (Think back to the story about the black dot.)

For example, maybe in your life you encountered someone like my coworker. The negative thought associated with that might be, *This person openly hated and discouraged me and that made me feel negatively about myself.*

That negative thought could be shifted by writing, "While that person hated and discouraged me, they taught me to be more open to the potential in each person, because they didn't take the time to find my potential—and that was a valuable lesson."

Now try one of your own.

Were you able to shift the filter from negative to positive easily, or do you need more practice? Think about how you can do this with a few thoughts every day to start embracing positivity and joy on a more consistent basis.

Chapter 7

ENGAGING EMPATHY AND EMBRACING MERCY

*True empathy isn't treating someone how you want to be
treated, it's treating them how they want to be treated.
—A Dr. Dan One-Liner (One that should be
familiar from earlier.)*

My goal and my heart in sharing the principles of empathy and mercy with you in this particular order is to help you build amazing leadership skills on that foundation. You will see how a strong foundation of knowledge based on the different topics we are covering in this book all relate to each other..

These two concepts have a unique relationship in the way they interact with each other. Once you learn about empathy and mercy as individual ideas, then we'll talk about how they team up to create amazing possibilities when you lead using them together.

Empathy alone is still important, and it can be life-changing for some. When we add mercy, which is the idea of taking action to support someone during a time of suffering, that's where we can really help them through whatever they're facing in that moment.

When it comes to thinking about empathy and how this concept can shape our leadership, the root for this behavior has to come back to the idea of each person being unique.

We've already established that every human is a unique gift that is waiting to be opened. And their distinct personalities and gifts also require us to make special considerations when we're thinking about how to empathize with them: how to put ourselves into their shoes and care about their circumstances, responsibilities, and feelings—each as unique as they are.

This is why I want to update what we think about when we hear the phrase "The Golden Rule." When people talk about this rule, they often say it means that we should treat others the way we want to be treated.

If you type "Where does the Golden Rule come from?" into a search engine, you will most likely be pointed to Jesus.

In Matthew 7:12, Jesus says, "So whatever you wish that men would do to you, do so to them; for this is the law and the prophets."

Jesus was saying that if you can manage to accomplish this one rule, you would be embracing the things that the law and the prophets taught in The Old Testament, a collection of knowledge that took over 1,000 years to gather.[6]

The way modern society has summed up this rule is missing something. It's neglecting to take the component of uniqueness into consideration.

Jesus didn't say, "Treat others as you want to be treated." He said, "So whatever you wish that men would do to you, do so to them" (Matthew 7:12).

In essence, Jesus is telling the listener to take into account what they would want so that they can then take into account what the person they're interacting with would want.

If we take Jesus' meaning into consideration, it becomes clear that the modern-day interpretation of "think about what *you* would want" leans on the selfish way today's society teaches us to focus solely on ourselves. We have to resist the temptation to accept this easy, feel-good answer to get to the bottom of what Jesus is really teaching: He invites us to consider how each person is a unique gift and should be treated in that way.

This is the true meaning of the Golden Rule. When we use empathy, we are thinking about how the other person wants to be treated. True empathy takes the main focus off ourselves and puts it on the other amazing and rare person along with their individual circumstances and preferences.

You see, the way you want to be treated isn't necessarily the way that someone else would want to be treated.

---

6   Dr. Michael A. Milton, "When Was the Bible Written? The History of God's Word," *Bible Study Tools*, February 21, 2019, https://www.biblestudytools.com/bible-study/topical-studies/when-was-the-bible-written.html.

The point of empathy is to have compassion for someone else, to put yourself into their shoes, understanding that everyone is going through different things in life. And because they are all unique, they will respond in varied ways to life events and daily situations.

There is also a measure of unconditional love required to make sure we are empathizing well. Earlier, we talked about how truly unconditional love means that we consider others and act to help them without expecting anything in return. In the story I'm about to share, there was a man who used empathy to put himself in my shoes when I literally had nothing that I could give him in return. And this event in my life is what helped me see how powerful empathy really is.

A Man Who Changed My Life by Putting Himself in My Shoes

When I first moved to Miami, Florida, from Peru, I was basically alone. I had a few cousins there, but they were busy attending to their own families, and they were in different phases of their lives. I understood that. But it didn't change the fact that I didn't have any friends. I was young and single, and I needed others to share my life with.

I managed to get an apartment, but I had no money to put anything inside of it. I was sleeping on an air mattress, and I had no cooking utensils or plates so I couldn't cook anything. At the same time, I didn't have the resources to buy takeout food.

There was this guy, Luchon, who I met through one of my cousins. (Yes, the same Luis "Luchon" who helped me understand that when people are purchasing a lottery ticket, they're buying a way to dream and hope.) He was older than me by 16 or 17 years, which meant he was an entire generation ahead of me. One day, Luchon invited me to his house to eat with his family. We spent all afternoon cooking, and I kept thinking, *Wow, this guy is a chef.*

I want you to understand, amazing reader, that Luchon and I had absolutely nothing in common at this point. He was a tough-looking guy who worked in a physically demanding job as a mechanical engineer. He had a beautiful family and decades of life experience.

I was a kid without a real piece of furniture to my name.

When we ate, I couldn't believe all the flavors I was tasting. And sure, I was hungry, but the food didn't just minister to my body, it ministered to my soul—along with the spiritual and relational companionship Luchon provided to me that night.

From that point on, Luchon would randomly call me and ask, "Hey, what are you doing?" I would answer honestly about my meager pantry: "Well, I was getting ready to eat some bread and butter." He would immediately invite me to come over to eat. He would go completely out of his way to show me kindness and give me words of encouragement.

In the kitchen with Luchon making delicious food together

And now, all of these years later, he is having so much fun in celebrating the success I've been able to have in building a loving family and growing a business from almost nothing. Luchon still cheers me on every step of the way. Not too long ago, I was on a visit to Miami, and when Luchon and I talked, he told me how proud of me he was—with tears in his eyes.

This man who I looked up to, who showed me such kindness, now looks at me as a man in my own right, and he's proud of me. That means so much. Especially when I think back to how he watched me struggle through life as a young kid, trying to figure out how to build what I wanted from nothing.

What Luchon did for me by giving me friendship has shaped every part of my adult life. I was there in Miami, a broke kid who didn't have anything. And a guy I didn't really know opened his home to me. He put himself in my shoes. He took the time to look at my story, and he realized my circumstances and what *I* would want based on my uniqueness and what I needed. One time, early in our relationship, he told me, "You're basically here alone, you have no one." But he didn't leave me in that state.

It was an unlikely friendship, but after all of these years, he still comes to visit and stays with my family in Wisconsin. He brings a suitcase full of his cooking utensils and cooks the dishes my wife, my kids, and I love the best.

Luchon is part of my family. When the two of us first started spending time together, he was a complete stranger. But because he saw me and put himself in my shoes, he was able to help me.

This is what true empathy is. And the impact Luchon had on my life has been profound, because he allowed empathy to lead his actions. He thought about what I needed even though I had nothing to offer in return but friendship. For him, that was more than enough. This is what is possible when you embrace empathy as a leader, whether that's at home, in your community, or at work.

And that's why as leaders, we need to know what empathy is and how to use it to help those around us.

The Mark of Empathy

Being able to use empathy as a leader is vital, but not everyone is willing to use it. Why? Real empathy takes work. In order to truly put ourselves into someone else's circumstances, we have to get to know them, which includes finding out what their situation is. We have to understand that since we are all unique, when things happen and we go through situations, we will each respond differently.

Empathy means employing compassion for others and where they are, understanding they will have unique responses to the things life throws at them. So before we get too much into what empathy is, let's take a look at a few additional concepts that will give us deeper context.

First, I said that empathy means employing compassion, but what do I mean when I use the word compassion? I gave you a few hints in the previous chapter. When we care about the sufferings of others and take their circumstances into consideration, that is true compassion. And it helps us to work with purpose to give others the benefit of the doubt. If we don't use compassion with empathy, we won't be able to truly put ourselves into the shoes of others, because we won't be curious about what shoes they're actually in.

There's another word that fits into this conversation that you might be wondering about: sympathy. I want to clarify that while empathy and sympathy are often used interchangeably, they are *not* interchangeable. Even though they have seemingly similar meanings, the results of each concept are dramatically different.

Empathy is centered on wanting to understand someone else's perspective about their situation so that you can support them, meaning there is action involved. Sympathy is just a feeling of sorrow you have for someone else about their circumstances that is still rooted in *your own* perspective. This difference is so big that, in some languages, they have a different word for "sorry" that means "I'm sorry with you and am by your side," which displays empathy, as opposed to "I'm sorry for you," which displays sympathy. We can sum up the difference between empathy and sympathy by pointing out that while empathy is active, sympathy is passive.

To take things a step further, next-level empathy also means embracing mercy on their behalf when they make mistakes (more on that in a minute).

As a leader, whether you're at a seven-figure company or at home with your spouse and children, you have a lot of people you need to get to know. And with family members, you have to build a much deeper knowledge of each person.

In previous chapters, we've discussed the importance of taking the time to understand the gifts and talents of others. This also means thinking about how they would want to be treated, taking into consideration what their skills actually are. Maybe you have someone who is amazing at typing, but they don't like doing data entry. You could put them in a position that uses their typing skills without having them sitting at a desk, entering data all day, every day.

You can also use empathy to frame those gifts and talents, which will help you become a more efficient and dynamic leader. But this requires investing the only resource that you can't make more of: your time.

And that can be difficult since we're surrounded by a culture that tells us to prioritize our own wants and desires first and foremost.

Empathy vs. Me, Me, Me

The first step to being more empathetic is to care enough to understand the other person (which we labeled earlier as compassion). When you care to understand and know those around you, that's when you can build relationships in a way that allows you to use empathy. There is a problem, though: We live in a selfish society in which we tend to think and talk a lot about ourselves.

But leadership depends upon us having strong relationships in our lives, because if there is no one around to lead, we can't be effective leaders. And these relationships cannot be created solely with the goal of building up our egos or positions. They need to be centered on building up others by desiring to understand them and their gifts. Selfish motives won't create the kind of long-lasting bonds like the one that was forged between me and Luchon, who was selfless in his care of me.

When we focus too much on ourselves, we think that happiness is just about us.

But as you see in my friendship with Luchon, he is now finding immense joy in the success I've had. He's walking beside me in my story. He's not only following along, he's part of what I'm doing.

Having a selfish mentality destroys relationships. This is true in every relationship, whether it's with a friend, a family member, your partner, or with someone in the workplace. And in order to confront the selfish attitudes that appear at work and at home, we have to realize which powerful tools come into play when we try to treat others the way *they* want to be treated (instead of how *we* would want to be treated). Empathy will drive us to take actions based on the feelings and situations of others, giving us compassion for their uniqueness. That is when we will be able to walk in their shoes.

Take a moment to reflect: What is currently shaping your own mentality when it comes to leading others around you? Are you being influenced by the selfishness modern culture promotes, or are you acting based on empathy?

Now, let's dive a bit deeper into the meaning and power of compassion. Without compassion, empathy cannot exist.

The Risk of Indifference and How Compassion Fights Back

If we want to see the way that building unique empathy (which takes into consideration the person's specific gifts, talents, and feelings) can transform the lives of those we lead, we have to start by confronting something that is the result of selfishness: indifference.

Indifference, which happens when you neglect to care about someone or something that's been entrusted to you, is destructive. It destroys not only relationships, but also people.

Indifference doesn't act on behalf of others. It doesn't consider how a unique soul and gift of a person wants to be treated. When someone becomes indifferent, this causes them to turn inward. Indifference creates isolation. And leadership can never happen in isolation.

The only way to combat indifference is with love: to love by showing compassion to others.

Compassion takes three things. First, we have to notice that something is going on with someone around us. Second, we have to care about what is happening with that person. Third, we have to do something to help with what that person is going through, and it needs to cost us something.

When we love others by showing them compassion, this is extremely powerful. Let's take a look at how compassion works as we love others by caring for them in a way that promotes empathy and discourages indifference.

First, we need to notice that something is going on with someone in our life—someone we have a relationship with. The only way we can do this is by refusing to engage with indifference. Noticing what is going on in the lives of others takes care through attention.

Second, we need to do something about what we've noticed. This means thinking about what the other person needs, like when Luchon realized I needed time with him and his family. And he recognized I literally needed food.

Third, we have to be willing to pay whatever that action costs us—and it *should* cost us something if it's really going to help that other person.

When we look at Luchon's presence in my life, it definitely cost him time and resources. His compassion brought me into those deeply relational moments with his family, and he spent money and time caring for me through the purchase and preparation of food.

So often as humans, we are experts at pointing out the problems around us. But we can't only use love-fueled compassion to care for those around us. We need to find solutions for those problems too.

One big related problem happens when I don't care for and love myself first. If I am indifferent toward myself, I won't be able to care for others in a positive way. In chapter 5, we talked about lighting your own candle before you could share that light, and the concept is just as applicable here. If you can't be compassionate to yourself, you will have a hard time being compassionate to anyone else.

Next, consider our obligations to our families. If we're out trying to save the world and neglecting our families, that isn't going to work.

And when it comes to our professional lives, the next group of people to look after are our teams. So the order needs to be: me, my family, and my team. But how many times are we tempted to look at "me" and what I want based on my ego and then stop there?

How often does it happen that when we do think about ourselves, we neglect to love ourselves with empathy and compassion? That requires showing ourselves forgiveness, grace, and mercy; and when we do, that's when we can begin to embrace change.

So what is mercy? How does it team up with compassion and empathy to help us make our own lives and the lives of those around us better?

Compassion Requires Mercy

Many years ago, I had a profound moment as I studied the word "mercy" and thought about how the concept fit into my life.

The Latin word that we find for mercy is *misericordia*, which comes from the words *misereri* and *cor*, respectively meaning "misery" and "heart." This literally means that your heart is close to the misery of others, to their suffering.

As leaders, both at work and at home, mercy encourages us to have our hearts close to the misery of those around us—our family members and the people on our work teams.

We're entrusted with those around us and have the opportunity to look at them as the people we serve, these unique ones with whom God has entrusted us.

This means we are compelled to use our talents in the service of others, but without empathy and mercy, we cannot effectively use our talents.

I want you to understand, though, that mercy *doesn't* mean that we should actively seek out suffering for suffering's sake. While misery is a part of mercy, it is in an effort to help others, not to torture ourselves so that we can amplify our own pain.

Mercy is active. So it is not the same as pity, which is where you say, "Too bad for them," and move on.

When you engage mercy on behalf of someone else, you enter into their misery to show them that you understand their need for support during a difficult time. And the way you show them that is by choosing to *do* things for them. You are choosing to show them compassion by caring about their circumstances. Whether that's being a listening ear, taking some tasks off their plate so that they can have time to process what they're going through, or investing in other ways to support them.

MERCY MEANS DOING.

Empathy, compassion, and mercy are at the very heart of servant leadership, and all of them are active. When you put yourself in the shoes of others, use compassion to understand and respond to their struggles and suffering, and work to recognize and support their gifts—this is where everything comes together.

However, we have to be mindful about a temptation that arises here. Sometimes we want to offset any rejection we might feel from people we have relationships with, and that will motivate us to show empathy and mercy to them. But in this case, it isn't unconditional. We are essentially saying, "I will be empathetic to you, but you must show me validation for my feelings and care for me in return." When we use empathy, compassion, or mercy in order to get love back from another person, it isn't real if it is conditional.

For example, imagine if one day your manager comes in and asks about something they know you are struggling with. They listen to you and offer you some solutions. They tell you that they are going to support you. But then, the next day, they come back into your office and tell you about an emotional struggle *they* have so that you will acknowledge their difficulties. They ask you for validation in a direct way, demanding that you fulfill their emotional need since they offered to help fix your problem. That is not empathy, compassion, or mercy: It's manipulation. Strings are attached.

Choosing to care for someone else by showing them compassion motivated solely by trying to fill the hole, which rejection from other people has caused in your life, will never lead to true satisfaction.

True fulfillment can only come by acting without hoping for anything in return.

Like Luchon did when he put himself in my shoes by asking, "How would I feel if I lived in a city alone, far away from my family?"

To be honest, that first night in my apartment in Miami was a total shock. I didn't have a single plate. Not a fork. Not even a real bed. And no friends to bring me dinner on move-in day.

But Luchon showed me love through his compassion. It wasn't just that he made me amazing food when I was hungry. He wanted to build a friendship, which I really needed. He also showed me admiration and encouraged me, telling me that I was capable of doing great things. He's one of the people who helped me learn about positivity, which changed my life. He called me a smart kid when I didn't always feel like one.

Luchon showed me love through his compassion for me. And he actively showed me mercy by opening his heart to my misery, my challenges. But he went beyond treating me how he would have wanted to be treated, using the Golden Rule: Luchon looked at how *I* would want to be taken care of as a young bachelor living alone; that's what he gave me through his offer of friendship, family, and food.

And the relationship we have now is so strong because of all his selfless acts on my behalf. Luchon has been a leader in my life now for many years. By using empathy, compassion, and mercy like he did, you can become an impactful leader like him.

How You Treat Them is How You'll Lead Them

Another one-liner that I often say is, "We fall in love because of the way the other person treats us." We come to love someone because of how they make us feel, and our feelings are informed by the way we are treated.

When I have conversations about this concept with my team, I tell them, "Your patient doesn't come here because of how great your dentistry is. It's all about how you treat that person. It's how you show empathy and love, and how you support them when they are in pain by having your heart be close to their misery—how you show them mercy. You might not be the best dentist in the world, but if you treat your patients with compassion, empathy, and truly care about them, these people will follow you and love you."

And the same is true about the people you lead, those on your professional teams.

However, I want to warn you about something I've seen many times. Empathy and mercy cannot be a strategy.

Even here in this book, you might have thought, *Well, Daniel, I came here to learn better leadership strategies, and now you're telling me I can't treat empathy and mercy as strategies. Why not?*

Because people will know if we aren't sincere. They will know if we don't truly care.

I believe there is too much strategy in the business world. What we really need is to embrace the privilege that we are blessed enough to be in positions of service.

What you might not have guessed about me is that when it comes to being a dental patient myself, I don't like it—at all. It's uncomfortable. It's painful. And when I think back to the dental practices that were being used 100 years ago, I cringe.

As far as doctors were concerned back then, there wasn't anything they could do about the pain their patients endured. So empathy wasn't warranted. They had these archaic tools and no anesthesia.

This lack of empathy demonstrated by dental practitioners back then is the reason we have so much stigma in the dental profession. This is why empathy and mercy are even more vital to our profession in dentistry today.

I'm sure you can think of reasons why empathy and mercy are vital in your industry, based on the past physical or emotional pain that the people your organization serves have been through.

In 2024, we had our traditional daylong company conference, and we asked the managers to do something new in preparation for our time together. Each one was asked to come up to say something good about a staff member of their choice—something that was special about that person.

One of the managers spoke about an assistant who would offer to hold the hands of any patients who were getting a shot. The feedback that the office received because of those selfless moments of handholding was both positive and encouraging. Why?

To serve others we need to say, "Yes, you are going to experience pain, and I understand. I'm here with you." This one assistant put their heart close to the misery of our patients by selflessly and physically holding their hands. And while this small act doesn't take away the pain of the patients, it does make them feel more okay with the pain—the shared experience makes the pain more manageable.

As far as dentistry goes, doing something like helping a patient get through a painful moment is a unique opportunity that can be transferred into the greater medical community. We have a responsibility and opportunity to comfort people.

In dentistry, we see that even patients who have had bad experiences with other professionals can be won over by the love they experience from our team. It's like the saying "kill them with kindness."

There are similar opportunities to show that caring in every kind of industry and workplace. Of course, when we tie our identity into what we do, there is a tendency to feel upset if we internalize what someone else thinks about our profession.

For example, if you are a lawyer and someone comes to you for help saying, "I'm here, but I hate lawyers," there is potential for you to get angry.

However, we can also engage our empathy in that type of situation to try to put ourselves in the shoes of that person to understand that their attitude is a result of something they've been through.

That is one of the best things about empathy: It helps us see others in a more positive light based on their unique humanity. None of our feelings were created in total isolation. It is through relationships, a critical part of being human, that our life experiences are shaped—and not all of us have had supportive relationships.

When we interact with people who are experiencing anger or mistrust, we can remind ourselves that empathy means we consider more than just this present moment. We also have the opportunity to think about what happened in their past that has shaped their response in that moment.

Ultimately, when we talk about empathy, compassion, and mercy, we can realize that the benefits we see from bringing these attitudes into our relationships can go so much further past the professional spaces we exist in. For example, at home, the ways we serve the people inside of our families will show an immeasurable amount of love and care.

We can show empathy and mercy to every person around us. That is how powerful these concepts are.

We have unique opportunities to use the true meaning of the Golden Rule to meet each person around us where *they* want to be met. We can take action through empathy to put ourselves in the shoes of others by caring for them with compassion. And we can use mercy to enter into their sufferings with our actions to support them through difficult moments.

This is why when empathy, compassion, and mercy are used together, they have the power to shape our leadership into something unstoppable. This not only impacts the mission and vision we have for our business, but builds up each unique gift of a person that has been entrusted to us.

Summary

- In Matthew 7:12, Jesus' golden rule invites us to consider how each unique person would want to be treated.
- Empathy means working to understand someone's feelings and circumstances—it takes effort and intention.
- True empathy treats others the way *they* want to be treated.
- Luchon showed me empathy by recognizing my loneliness and offering me unconditional love that changed my life.
- Empathy takes time, and a self-focused culture often resists that. But selfishness damages relationships.
- Mercy is compassion in action, being moved by others' misery and choosing to help.

- Love without empathy and mercy is hollow. Real fulfillment comes from selfless action.
- Empathy, compassion, and mercy aren't tactics—they reflect a deeper way of living.
- When we recognize each person's unique story, we're better able to show true empathy.

Actions to Take

Next, journal through your own definitions of empathy, compassion, and mercy while considering the following questions:

- What is my own definition of empathy? When has someone shown me empathy like Luchon did for Daniel? How did that change the way I felt about the situation I was in?
- What is my own definition of compassion? When has someone been compassionate to me in a way that changed my perspective? My life?
- What is my own definition of mercy? When have I experienced mercy without condition from someone in my life? How did that change the way I felt about myself in that situation?
- How can I use empathy, compassion, and mercy to impact the people on my team as a leader?
- How can I use empathy, compassion, and mercy to encourage the people I lead in my family or community?

Set the Empathy Standard

Use the following assessment to determine your current approaches to empathy. Answer yes or no for each prompt. Then, for each question where you answer "no," think about how you can better embrace the concept associated with the question.

1. When someone has a problem with a person in my profession, I can distance myself enough to think about how their experiences caused them to form that opinion.

2. If I see someone struggling, I am confident that I can take action by putting myself in their shoes to better understand their situation.

3. Feeling sorry for people isn't enough. I know that in the relationships I have, I should be motivated to take action to help.

4. Lighting my own candle first is important, but that's not where I stop.

5. Although I know it won't be comfortable, I am willing to put my heart next to the misery of the people I have relationships with.

Chapter 8

THE HARMONY
TEAMWORK CREATES

The most powerful thing you can say to
someone is "I believe in you."
—A Dr. Dan One-Liner

When I was 14 years old, something unforgettable happened in my life. The negative identity I had given myself was about to be turned upside down by one thoughtful and purposeful teacher.

You see, growing up, I always thought I was a bad student. As I progressed through school, I was told this many times by my teachers. And eventually, I put this idea on and wore it as part of my identity.

Then one day, my ninth-grade chemistry teacher, Mr. Manuel Serra, returned my test marked with a failing grade and asked me to meet him in his office during recess.

"Why is it that a smart kid like you is failing so horribly in this subject?" he asked. "How are you doing in your other classes?"

"I'm not doing well," I said.

"Well, I want to meet with your parents. Please tell them to get in touch with me."

In that moment, I couldn't help but think about how hard I had worked to keep my parents from finding out about my bad grades. And now my teacher was about to parade my failure in front of them. At the same time, I knew I couldn't avoid talking to them about my schoolwork any longer, but I didn't have to be the one to tell them I was failing—Mr. Serra could be the one to do that. It was a small relief that I wouldn't have to look them in the eyes when they found out.

Later that afternoon, when both of my parents were home, I went to them and said, "I don't know why, but one of my teachers wants to talk to both of you."

The difficult part for me was that I wasn't in that meeting. My parents went in to talk to Mr. Serra, and I'm still—all these years later—not exactly sure what he said to them. What they did tell me is that Mr. Serra thought I was very smart and I just didn't realize it. He had also offered to come to my house twice a week to tutor me for free.

My parents had said yes and thanked him.

Looking back, I realize that my parents would have not been able to afford to get me a tutor, and this chemistry teacher's free offer of help was exactly what I had needed.

Mr. Serra would come two, sometimes three, days per week and mentor me. He taught me how to rethink my approach to learning, how to study, and how to rip the label off myself that said "bad student." I had freely accepted that label so many years earlier. Even though Mr. Serra was three years older than my dad, he became my friend. He talked with me like we were the same age. I could tell him anything that was going on in my life.

This man did so many amazing things for me, but the biggest gift he gave me was belief in myself. When we first met, he said, "You're very smart. Why are you failing?" I laughed out loud because I thought he was crazy. But what he noticed about me was real: He saw in me what I couldn't see in myself.

Mr. Serra told me, "I believe in you," in both his words and actions.

Fast forward to my present life, and recently, my son asked me, "Do you think that Mr. Serra knows how much he changed not only your life, but our lives? That what he did for you affected our family so much?"

That question made me think. My son understood that the way Mr. Serra shaped my life had directly affected our family, and him, my son, in such a positive way.

"I don't think so, son," I said in response, knowing that Mr. Serra had passed away.

I often think, *I wish Mr. Serra could see me now and how I've been able to help others with the help he gave me.*

Mr. Serra at a school function

After Mr. Serra died, I saw many notes from past students he helped, just like me. I guess each year, he'd take on one student to help. When I was in ninth grade, *I* was that privileged student. I cannot describe in words what a blessing he was to me. And my son is right: Mr. Serra dramatically impacted not only my life, but everyone in my family and on my professional team.

And as a leader, you can have that same impact on the people in your life.

The Power of "I Believe in You"

The story of Mr. Serra can help us be better leaders in every arena of life. I think it comes down to a seemingly simple concept that is anything but simple: People need to be told that someone believes in them.

Another example of what impact this can create is found within the Dream Team. No, not the 1992 US Olympic Men's Basketball Team. The other one: Jesus and his disciples.

When we look at the different accounts of the four Gospels—Matthew, Mark, Luke, and John—and later in Acts when Paul joined the group after Jesus ascended into heaven, we can see that Jesus didn't choose people for His team the way a CEO might have chosen.

His chosen team members were unique people with their own strengths and imperfections. We know that Peter ended up denying Jesus as His path to the cross and death played out. Matthew was a tax collector, which meant he wasn't someone that the Jewish community of that time wanted around; he would have been viewed as someone who acted against his own culture. Simon was referred to as a zealot because of his hatred for the Romans.[7]

And yet, they had the makings of a team that would be able to influence the entire world.

Why? How?

---

7   Jim Van Vurst, "Franciscan Inspirations: Jesus Chooses His 12 Apostles," *Franciscan Media*, March 23, 2024, https://www.franciscanmedia.org/franciscan-spirit-blog/franciscan-inspirations-jesus-chooses-his-12-apostles/.

Because Jesus met those men in the midsts of their messy humanity. He knew they weren't perfect. But at the same time, Jesus saw their unique gifts. And He worked to help each of them understand that He believed in them in spite of these imperfections. This is how powerful "I believe in you" is.

In the case of Jesus, His belief in these men who became His disciples literally changed the world. And even though these disciples were a team, Jesus also ministered to each one of them individually. And that's how Mr. Serra worked with me.

So how can you use this life-changing concept to shape your family and your organization, one person at a time? Let's find out.

Just One Person

By now, we know that every person is a unique gift. And in chapter 7, we saw that empathy allows us to step into the shoes of each wonderful and amazing person. It is only when we truly understand and embrace the specific circumstances and gifts of each person that we can find harmony inside our homes and teams.

When it comes to changing our families and teams one person at a time, there is another step that is required.

We must believe that we can trust in other people's capabilities. And, to take this belief one step further, when we say "I believe in you" to the person we're leading, we need to mean it. And show them we mean it. The action required then is to give that person an opportunity to show you that you're right in your belief, correct in choosing to believe in them.

When you tell someone that you believe in their ability to do whatever it is they have the knowledge and skills to do, and then you delegate a related responsibility to them, you are empowering them! This is life-giving to that person.

Being able to take belief and turn it into visible trust in others is a vital skill for any leader to have, whether you're supporting your VP of operations or your teenage daughter.

Trust is one of the highest gifts you can give to someone who you want to lead effectively. And in order to begin, I want you to think about that *one* person you want to help first. Who would your belief most serve today? And why? Think back to how Mr. Serra recognized I *could* be a good student and believe in myself; he gave me his belief and the skills to take action so I could thrive. Each valuable endeavor in life starts with *just one person.*

As we talk about the idea of "I believe in you," maybe you have or haven't heard that phrase from someone in your life. If you have, I want to remind you that it's true. If you haven't, I'm so sorry, and I want you to know that I really do believe in you. You wouldn't be here, reading this book about how to make the world a better place by leading, if you weren't interested in helping others. And that confirms to me that I am *right* to believe in you.

When I work with my team, I make sure to say "I believe in you" often to them, both collectively and individually. And I encourage them to say it to the people who they lead. But you might be surprised how many times I hear back, "Dr. Dan, I have never been told that someone else believed in me and that I am worthy of being trusted with something."

Isn't that heartbreaking? I wish that wasn't the case, but as leaders, we have a chance to change this by telling people we believe in them.

In fact, as leaders, it is our *responsibility* to look for and encourage other people's virtues (their good character) and talents. Sometimes, this will be speaking directly to that person about their amazing talents. Other times, you might want to have one of your leaders, someone you know who has a connection with this person, be the one who identifies their virtues and talents with them.

You might also be wondering, "Which *one* person am I supposed to start with?"

I don't have all the answers, but my first instinct is for you to make sure you're telling your family members you believe in them. These are the most important relationships in your life, and they should be your top priority.

At work, I would suggest choosing someone that you know needs help. Mr. Serra saw that I was struggling—that I had identified myself as a dumb kid. But he also saw my potential and reached out.

Once Mr. Serra invested time and effort into helping me, the difference was night and day; I became an excellent student. I ended up graduating high school as one of the top people in my class. That was truly because of the way Mr. Serra believed in me, and that belief changed the way I viewed myself.

I was able to get academic scholarships that helped me on my path, and I attribute all of that to the way Mr. Serra transformed my life.

If you change one life, you can change the world—like Mr. Serra did—one year at a time with one student at a time. In addition to my son's recognition of Mr. Serra's far-reaching impact beyond my life, the social media tributes I found from his past students are proof of his far-reaching influence.

What if you took this approach with one person for one year in your professional organization, and then taught that person to do the same? How would that transform your company? How would this kind of work heal the hurts that so many people on your team probably have suffered? Maybe no one in your organization has told them that you all believe in them. Imagine the impact that your belief and your trust in them to take action could have.

I believe in you. And you can do this—one person at a time.

But what happens when that person you've put your belief in makes a mistake? What then?

Team Up with the Person, Not the Problem

The heading of this section is another official Dr. Dan One-Liner that I say regularly. Why? So often we want to feel all the emotions in life—the anger, the frustration, and sometimes, even the rage. And when it comes to work mistakes and interpersonal issues, the potential for all of those feelings can be amplified. Because we want to embrace those emotions, we often team up with the problem instead of the person.

Why does this happen? Think back to chapter 6 where we talked about how society *wants* us to emphasize the negative, and you'll understand why workroom gossip mills exist.

So what is a positive way to deal with mistakes? Let's take a look. A mistake can occur when something that was supposed to happen doesn't. Or an action that was meant to be completed a certain way doesn't meet the standard that's been previously established. Deadlines get missed. The gluten-free muffin basket you ordered contains nothing but gluten.

When it comes to building effective teams that solve difficult issues consistently, teaming up with the problem can be a big—well—problem.

And when it comes to loving and leading your family well, making the small change to team up with the person over the problem can transform everything.

To team up with family, the action you take might be extremely practical. At home there are often different tasks or chores we assign to help keep things running smoothly. But sometimes, in the midst of the business of life, we forget to complete those tasks. Forgetting is one kind of mistake that happens.

For example, you might notice that your spouse has forgotten to grab the passports for everyone in the family on the way to the international flight. Yes, that is a mistake. But if you get upset, that isn't going to change the circumstances. The best action to take in that situation is to go back and get the passports and to *not* give them a lecture. When you take action to help them correct the problem, you show the other person that you value them even when they make mistakes. And also that you're there to help.

Or you can get angry and yell at them for being forgetful. But that's teaming up with the problem. They will think that if they forget to take out the trash again, which is a mistake, you'll yell at them. This is motivating them out of fear.

But if you encourage them to remember by acknowledging how busy they are and that you took care of it this time, you're teaming up with them—the person. This makes a huge difference because they will be motivated to take the trash out next time from a place of love. And love beats out fear every time.

A lot of the time at work, people are scared to make mistakes because they don't want to receive disciplinary action or be fired. And as managers, we often want to protect our team members and our customers or clients from the mistakes that others make. So when the inevitable happens and something goes wrong, we get mad at ourselves for not better protecting ourselves or our team members from those mistakes.

Then, we might think, *I don't want to trust someone else with this because mistakes can cost valuable time, and it will be faster if I just do it myself.*

If leaders continue to think that way, it takes trust out of the equation.

When we refuse to trust someone else with what they've been trained to do because of the mistakes they *will* make (no one is immune to messing things up here and there), we are teaming up with the problem. And it's a future problem that hasn't even happened yet.

If, on the other hand, we lead from a place of being selflessly invested in the success of the people around us, regardless of what our long-term relationship will look like, that's when we are teaming up with the person. Let me explain.

I hear some leaders say, "Well, I don't want to invest in training this person because they might leave."

This is evident, especially in the dental industry, where some contracts say that if the doctor leaves a clinic, they are required to pay the employer back for their training. In my opinion, that should never be the case.

If a doctor is learning how to do something better, and they end up going to another group or clinic and using those skills to help their patients, I'm still winning. That's how I look at it.

Many leaders won't give their team leaders or managers the training or guidance they need based on fear that this person will leave. But that approach is never going to help the team build better skills they can use to better serve each other, their patients, clients, or customers.

As leaders, though, it's our duty to empower people. Helping them take action is so much better than building a vague strategy to improve such-and-such profitability. Building trust with your team members naturally leads to greater profitability. When you take action from a place of confidence, doing the right thing by providing training will make a tangible difference. This is in direct contrast to refusing to take action based on fear—where the result is withholding the time and resources your team really needs to succeed.

Let's look at examples of each: teaming up with the problem and then teaming up with the person.

Laura double-books a cleaning slot. Suddenly the team realizes they are going to be behind all day if they don't rebook one of the people—and fast. In response, Laura's manager screams at her in the back room, where everyone, including the patients, can hear what's going on. With a red face and slouched shoulders, Laura comes out and asks if one of the patients would be able to come into the office the next day. Out of concern for Laura, one of the patients agrees, but they never go back to that office since the screaming manager made them extremely uncomfortable.

Laura's manager teamed up with the problem, not the person.

Now imagine that the same thing happens at a different office, and Sandy is the one who created the double-booking. Her manager notices the problem and walks with Sandy into the waiting room to support Sandy while she explains the situation to the patients. In the background, the team members are looking at the schedule to see how they can accommodate both patients if neither of them wants to come back the next day. And someone at the front office starts making calls to verify that everyone on the schedule that day can make it.

One of the patients has a flexible schedule and agrees they can come in the next day. And even if one of the patients hadn't been able to reschedule, the team was working to find solutions instead of getting angry at Sandy and shaming her for the mistake she made.

Sandy feels supported by her manager and her coworkers because they teamed up with her, not the problem. And the next time she makes an appointment, she will double-check that the slot is free—out of love for her team and not wanting them to feel stressed or rushed. This approach is so much stronger than what Laura's manager tried to do by using anger to create fear in Laura.

Once you realize how to team up with the person, there are additional things you can do to build an even more supportive environment at work.

As you continue to build trust with a team member, you can think about next steps, like asking the person you're working with, "How can I help you get to where you want to go?" Imagine what my life would be like if Mr. Serra hadn't worked with me on skills outside of chemistry, like learning and studying. His belief was the first piece, but then he worked to give me the skills I needed to succeed. And he supported me as I put each of those new concepts into action in school in real time.

That's why I always start with belief. I tell all of the dentists who work with me: "You are qualified for this job." I don't care if they're just out of school or have ten years of experience. They passed all the tests, their National Boards, and that means they are capable of taking action.

At the same time, I consistently want to make sure they have the tools and training they need to improve. I give them opportunities to learn new skills and then use them in real time on the job.

My team is constantly hearing from me that today we have to be better than yesterday, and tomorrow we have to be better than today.

The next time you realize there has been a mistake, take a moment to pause and ask yourself, "Am I going to team up with the problem and get super upset, or am I going to team up with the person and help them find a solution?" I find that this question makes all the difference—whether it's in an effort to build a better team or to create a more loving family.

Which Mistakes Need Correction?

I hope that by now you've noticed that I don't just encourage my team and my readers to embrace positivity: I work to grow in positivity myself.

But there will be moments when the person you're leading makes a mistake that needs to be corrected. You can stay positive in that moment even if what happened needs to be addressed.

So how do you know when it's time to correct? It all goes back to your values and mission.

In the second chapter, we talked about what it means to have a mission and how to think about your values in the light of that mission. Here, I want to show you what needs to happen when a team member makes a mistake that is related to character: one that goes against the company mission or breaks the company's values.

On our team, we work to build the attitude of a family. This doesn't mean that coworkers will become family members. That isn't possible because in your family, you can't fire a sibling. When I talk about the attitude of a family, I would say that we need to act in a way that shows others we only want the best for them—that we're there to support them as they grow in their gifts and embrace their uniqueness.

When I first meet with new team members, I tell them, "If you don't feel like someone you're around wants the best for you, then you need to let me know." Or the leaders in my organization will tell their team members the same thing and say, "Let Dr. Dan know."

For example, at one point, we heard from a team member that someone else on the team was making condescending comments to others—on two different occasions, which showed it was a pattern of behavior.

This particular team member had said something discouraging to others about how they lacked efficiency. This statement wasn't supportive: It was selfish. Each team member's job is to literally help the people around them. Yes, the other team members had made mistakes, but the person who had made the condescending comments was teaming up with the problem and not giving solutions to their fellow team members .

Since something similar had happened more than once, this felt like a trend, and I knew we needed to do something about it.

I brought this person into a meeting with me and my leadership group. I asked the team member whether the information I had was correct and she said it was. I was glad that she was being honest. But I also needed her to know that her behavior wasn't acceptable. I said, "You cannot act this way. You are representing our organization and you know the values we have for our group. You need to align with those values. Let me ask you, why do you think this happened?"

In humility, she acknowledged her mistake and said that her actions were completely unacceptable. I asked her what she thought she was going to do in response, and she said that she needed to apologize to the people she had been condescending toward. And she was true to her word and apologized.

As the leader of our organization, I didn't want anyone else to handle this. It had to be me.

Before I had the meeting with this individual, I personally called the team members who had shared the related information with our managers and told them I was going to do something. Then I checked back in with the affected people to make sure everything was okay. They said they had received an apology and everything was going well from that point on.

When we trust that if leadership grows, everyone else will too, we are able to establish the attitude of a family where we can grow from each others' success.

As leaders, it should always be our goal to keep learning and transforming our skills to increase our impact. And when we do that, we contribute to a culture at work that promotes growth in everyone.

The team member we spoke with who had been condescending to others learned this exact lesson in our meeting. She learned that by supporting those who were struggling with a task, she would ensure her own success, and the success of everyone in her work family.

But what if you find yourself in a workplace that doesn't seem to care about its values and mission being put in jeopardy by misaligned behavior? Leaders know that this happens, and it's worth talking about.

Toxic Work Environments

If you find that you are in a place where there is a leader (or multiple leaders) who want nothing more than to see you fail, that's not where you are going to succeed. Earlier, I mentioned that I think everyone should have the tools and training they need to grow and learn: to constantly improve. Unfortunately, not all people in positions of power agree with me.

If you find yourself in a situation where someone wants you to fail, this is an opportunity to choose to act with compassion. You might not know what happened to them that has caused them to behave that way, but I guarantee something happened.

At the same time, there is a difference between someone who is *waiting* for you to fail and someone who is *setting you up* to fail.

Waiting for you to fail means they aren't giving you the instructions, support, or information you need. This is when you can choose to respond to them with compassion based on the fact that you don't know why they behave that way.

However, when someone repeatedly shows you through their actions that they *don't* trust you to use your skills and talents to serve your team and that they are actively working to get you to fail in front of the team, this is setting you up to fail. That's when it's time to talk to their manager.

It is very unlikely that such a person will change on their own. Why? Because you know they are acting based on fear, which we talked about earlier. Either they are afraid of the future mistakes you could make that would reflect back on them, or they are anxious that you will leave after they invest in you with time and training. It could also be that they don't want you to level up and leave them behind. Or maybe they're afraid of you getting the attention they so desperately want.

And if their manager doesn't seem concerned with their behavior, then you know it's time to find an opportunity to work at a different place where you know that your values and those who are in leadership positions will be a better match.

But what happens when it's a team member who is toxic, and you realize that you need to say goodbye to them? How does that work?

Saying Goodbye Well

In leadership, as in life, there are moments when we need to say goodbye. If we can manage to do so well, we will be serving our values and our missions.

In my own organization, we do not fire people for their mistakes: That would be a mistake.

If someone is being careless or intentionally causing problems, that is one thing. But a mistake isn't necessarily a fireable offense. However, as you saw earlier, if someone is acting outside of our organization's values, that is an issue we want to address. And if we don't see changes from that person, that's when we part ways because it isn't a good fit for either party or the business

The attitude in a family that I mentioned earlier does not mean that we only do nice things for each other all the time. We also need to challenge each other. And as leaders, part of our responsibility is to encourage the team members we are entrusted to work with. We must guide them to become better at their gifts and to embrace new ones we notice that might take them outside of their comfort zones.

This is why, when we challenge team members who have stepped outside of our values, and we see no change from them, to keep things the same would be a disservice to everyone involved.

Even when you let someone go, you are doing it out of compassion. If you are making the choice to part ways with someone who isn't a good fit—not because you want to retaliate—this will give that person an opportunity to find the right position and place for them. And the failure they faced as part of this process can also ignite a positive change in them, so it's still a good and caring thing to do.

And now that you know how to encourage and interact with belief and trust, one person at a time, you'll be able to use your platform of leadership to inspire others with compassion and understanding, even when those inevitable mistakes happen. Jesus was able to work through the problems that Peter had during the time of the resurrection. Jesus teamed up with Peter, not the problem, and as a result, Peter became the first leader of the Church.

Imagine what could happen when you put belief and trust in a Peter inside your organization or inside your home. Now you know how to do that, and I believe you can!

In the next chapter, we're going to talk about what it means to be a servant leader, because choosing service and sacrifice has the potential to transform anyone into a meaningful leader.

Summary

- Hearing "I believe in you" can literally change someone's life. It did mine.
- The power of belief can transcend generations, which is what my son helped me realize when he said that Mr. Serra had changed *our* lives.
- When Jesus was forming His Dream Team, the disciples, He picked imperfect humans and met them where they were.
- When we trust someone, we are empowering them.
- You can change the world by changing one life.
- When we team up with the person instead of the problem, we can work through mistakes to find solutions.
- If team members are acting in a way that is outside your organization's values and mission, that needs to be addressed directly.

- Having someone *waiting* for you to fail is different than someone *setting you up* to fail. The first invites compassion, the second invites the involvement of that person's manager.
- When we choose to say goodbye to a team or need to say goodbye to a team member, there are still opportunities to act in positive, compassionate ways.

Actions to Take

Journal about the following prompts to help you realize where you've had a Mr. Serra in your corner and when you've been a Mr. Serra for someone else as you think about your life so far.

- When has someone else in your life made you feel supported? Who were they and what attributes and attitudes did they have? Make a list of your answers to this question. Were they kind? Did they give you their time in the form of training? And so on.
- Have you ever worked to support someone who needed to see your belief in them? How did that go? Are there any adjustments you would make based on what you learned in this chapter if you were to help someone like that again?

The Delegation Readiness Evaluation

When it comes to trusting those on your team, you need to show them trust in action by being able to delegate. Take the evaluation below to gauge where you are when it comes to your willingness to delegate. Write a "T" for True if you agree with the statement, or an "F" for False if you disagree. Then see the instructions after the statements to determine your results.

1. It would be faster if I just do everything myself instead of having to train someone else and then fix their mistakes.

2. If people were more competent, I wouldn't need to oversee things so closely.

3. The people being onboarded to my team aren't working with the same quality as I used to see when I was younger.

4. If there is a problem, the person responsible has to go. There isn't room for any human error on my team.

5. I can't trust people to help me because I feel like they're going to leave eventually.

If you answer three or more as "T" for True, think about how you can adjust your attitude to embrace trusting others based on what you learned in this chapter. And ask yourself how you would feel if your manager or leader thought these things about you. Would you be encouraged or discouraged?

Chapter 9

SERVICE AND SACRIFICES

Service is a way to happiness.
—A Dr. Dan One-Liner

If you look up different leadership models online, one of the methods you are bound to find is the servant leader approach. We see books, talks, and courses all about servant leadership. According to Google Trends, searches for the term "servant leadership" have gradually increased from 2004 to 2022 as the world has taken notice of this seemingly updated way to lead.[8]

However, this isn't really a new concept. We see Jesus teaching His disciples by modeling this style of leadership in the different Gospels. In John 13, we see what would be considered an extreme cultural example where Jesus takes on the role not just of a servant, but as the lowest level of servant. In His hands, He takes each foot of His 12 disciples, wiping and cleaning away the filth from the paths and roads, leaving every man with

---

8   "'Servant Leadership' Query," *Google Trends*, April 2, 2025, https://trends.google. com/trends/explore?date=all&geo=US&q=servant%20leadership&hl=en.

clean, unblemished skin. Beneath the towel wrapped around His waist, as He performs this service, His tunic turns from light to dark as the dust particles collect in the cloth.

This all happens while the disciples watch and wait for their turn, not believing what they're seeing.

Finally, the scene becomes too much for Peter, who tells Jesus that his feet will never be washed by Him. But Jesus' response blows Peter away.

> Peter said to him, "You shall never wash my feet." Jesus answered him, "If I do not wash you, you have no part in me." ...Peter said to him, "Lord, not my feet only but also my hands and my head!" Jesus said to him, "He who has bathed does not need to wash, except for his feet, but he is clean all over; and you are clean..."
>
> –John 13:8-10

Even in this short scene, we can see that Jesus had a style of servant leadership so impactful that Peter's response goes from resistance to enthusiasm as he asks Jesus to clean his hands and head as well as his feet.

Servant leadership happens when the person who is leading acts in humility—willing and even excited to do whatever the job or task is—not thinking of what they need to do through the lens of their elevated position or office.

Think about this. Have you ever seen a CEO doing something like what Jesus does in this story? Imagine that the members of a company's C-suite got together and deep cleaned every team member's pair of shoes. That would be grueling work that left them covered in dirt. They definitely wouldn't look or feel as polished as they normally do sitting behind their desks. Imagine with me for a moment how the members of this team would react to such a bold act of humility and service. Would it endear them to their leaders? I think the result we see with Jesus and His disciples points to *yes*.

In this chapter, I invite you to imagine what servant leadership on this level would look like today. Is it asking simple, heartfelt questions? Is it investing time in helping someone based on what they say they need? How can we follow the example Jesus sets in these verses?

One of the things that often gets overlooked in this scene is the intimacy of Jesus in His leadership. He is being of service to His disciples in a situation where they are vulnerable and so is He. This foot-cleaning ritual is an act that only happens in the privacy of a home. And it shows a great deal of respect for the person who is having their feet washed. Jesus meets His disciples in this intimate moment to care for them in a practical way that showcases His love for each one of them and emphasizes the bond they share.

Servant leaders sacrifice their time to do what needs to be done for the benefit of those around them. It is important to make this time for others, like we saw in chapters 7 and 8. Time is the only thing we can't make more of, and when we invest it in others, that shows our care for them. Servant leaders also look for opportunities to support team members to develop their gifts, like we saw in chapter 8. Most importantly, servant leaders make decisions based on loving the people around them, regardless of their position.

When we lead those around us—whether at home or at work—servant leadership demands an equal level of care to follow the example of Jesus and His same attitude of service.

And if we want to search for Jesus' opinion outside of John 13, we can also look to Mark 10:45, which says, "For the Son of man also came not to be served but to serve, and to give His life as a ransom for many." In this verse, Jesus makes it clear that even though He could have come here to *be* served as a leader, He actually came to serve *others*. And also inEphesians 6:7-9, which reads, "Rending service with a good will as to the Lord and not to men, knowing that whatever good any one does, he will receive the same again from the Lord, whether he is a slave or free." This verse reminds us that we have a greater mission in our spiritual lives that can expand to every area of life—that in serving others we are actually serving God. We might read these verses and think about how amazing they are in the context of religion, but there is so much more for us as leaders within these words.

Each of us is extremely fortunate to have a professional service in the form of our career where we can use our gifts to serve others. We might also be blessed with a family responsibility that allows us to serve the people we care about most.

It doesn't matter if you are a dentist, a doctor, a mother, or an uncle: You, too, can have the same attitude of service Jesus had.

But what is the reason we would want to adopt this servant leadership style in the first place? The answer is that when we put the needs of others ahead of ourselves, that is the real way to happiness: Not only for the people we serve, but for us as well. This is the kind of leadership that inspires others to sacrifice and serve the people around them.

Service and sacrifice (which are both defined below) are qualities that can start with leadership and easily spread to every person in an organization or in a family. Think about how Jesus washed the feet of the disciples. He did that to show them His love. It wasn't something He was required to do. Jesus did this to show the disciples He was willing to serve them, to sacrifice His time and dirty His clothes—even His position of power. We see that even more clearly in Jesus' sacrifice on the cross.

In this chapter, we're going to take a look at how the two attitudes of service and sacrifice can totally transform the way you lead.

What is service?

Service is love in action. It means that you spend your energy and effort on behalf of someone else in order to support them and make their lives better.

Service can be as simple as filling up your spouse's water bottle. It can also be as complicated as planning a trip to a wonderful place thousands of miles away to spend focused time away with your family—all with the intention to build up and cement your relationships with each other.

Service can also be something as seemingly small as making sure the office has a working coffee pot that allows all your team members access to the caffeine train to start their mornings off the way they prefer—with a hot cup of what they consider to be delicious in hand. It could also be something as simple as taking five minutes to really listen to someone who you know is going through something difficult at home.

A true act of service goes beyond the expected and shows intentional thought and care for someone else.

And now that we know what service is, let's move on to sacrifice.

What is sacrifice?

The most simple human need in life is love. We were created out of God's love and made to receive God's love. God *is* love. You might be wondering what love has to do with sacrifice. That's a great question.

I always tell my team and my kids: Service means sacrifice, sacrifice means love, and love means happiness.

Why is sacrifice love? Because there is an opportunity within sacrifice to show love. When we think about sacrifice, we also notice there is often a cost involved. Earlier, we saw Jesus putting Himself in the position of a servant so that He could clean the dirty feet of His disciples, but He actually came to this world for an even greater sacrifice.

When Jesus died on the cross, that was costly to Him in such an intense way that He cried out in pain, covered in sweat and blood. But His actions of sacrifice created a revolution that went around the world. In fact, many of us still experience the inspiration He caused through His sacrifice thousands of years ago. That is how powerful servant leadership is in the form of service and sacrifice.

Love means happiness because when we love others, when we serve and sacrifice for them, that brings happiness into our lives. This happiness comes from the fulfillment we experience when we are of service to the people around us.

Before I show you exactly what can happen when you lead by serving and sacrificing, let's take a look at what happens when you try to lead by entitlement, meaning making demands based on your own desires. This happens in direct contrast to wanting to serve and sacrifice for those around you in an intimate way like Jesus did.

Trying to Lead by Entitlement

Because I grew up in poverty, one of the main reasons I wanted to succeed in such an intense way was so that I could escape from having such limited resources. I didn't want to continue to face scarcity each and every day, and I definitely didn't want that for my family as we grew in number over time.

Even as God provided miracles that allowed me to purchase my first practice and to begin to build Mercy Dental Group, I kept looking ahead, waiting to eventually reach the point where I would have enough money so that I wouldn't have to work so hard.

The reality is when that finally happened, I incorrectly thought I didn't need to contribute at home anymore. I had gone out and made the money. It was entitlement that told me I was more important than anyone around me, including my family members. Once I started to give in to thoughts motivated by this entitlement, I suddenly felt entitled about everything. My time. My resources. Even my thoughts. I didn't want to have to *think* about what my family needed because any time away from work was my comfortable time, and difficult thoughts interrupted that comfort.

Soon I hired people to clean, and I was able to employ others so that I no longer had to do much when I wasn't working. What I really wanted to do once I had hit that number of "enough" in my head was to focus on my own desires.

To me this meant watching fútbol. And not just one game, but every game in the entire league that I loved—the Spanish League (La Liga)—no matter what time the matches aired or how many there were. Sitting down and drinking a beer without anyone, meaning my family, bothering me during my games was what I considered "making it." But my wife had a different idea of what I should be doing with my time.

At this point, you might be thinking, *Dr. Dan, spending all of your free time glued to the TV doesn't sound like anything you've taught us in this book*, and you're right. You see, even when I was deep into my fútbol phase, I was still teaching and preaching all the principles you're reading in this book right now. The 7 marks of leadership were still present during every onboarding process I did with new team members. And while I was trying to live the marks of leadership at work, I completely ignored them at home.

I call this time in my life a season of selective service, where I only did what *I* wanted to do, supported in this choice by the entitlement I felt.

Because the same successes I was having at work *weren't* happening at home, I spent a lot of hours in our family home engaged in "me time," avoiding confrontation. This caused a huge disconnect between me and my children, as well as frustration and deep disappointment for my wife, Scarlett.

If someone pointed out my failures at home, I would think, *They're being ungrateful. Can't they see how well I am providing for them each and every day?* But I wasn't truly sacrificing for my family. I wasn't serving them when I was at home.

As we're going to see in part 2 of the book, we often dedicate the most time and energy to the area of our lives where we feel most successful—and then we focus on the thing we're doing well to avoid the areas in our lives where we feel like we're failing. And that's exactly what I did with my work life to avoid the way I was failing at home

I thought my role was to go to work, come home, lay down, and watch fútbol while having a beer. In my heart, I told myself, *Your family is more than capable of figuring things out without you.* In the next chapter, you're going to see how wrong I was and how these actions were based on the entitlement I felt and took years to fix. There were serious divides that my selfish attitude created. But for now, I want you to know that even though I had everything I had ever wanted, I was still bitter, disappointed, and unhappy—all because of the entitled approach I was taking.

The life I had worked to build wasn't giving me the satisfaction I had hoped would follow, despite the professional success I had seen up until that point.

When I demanded respect and obedience because of how hard I worked away from home, my children resented me. The presence I brought into their lives wasn't one of connection or intimacy. I was a selfish person, demanding respect without giving it in return.

And when we try to lead businesses this way, we will never be able to inspire those around us. If we try to lead by entitlement, the only thing keeping the people around us is their paycheck—and that motivation will only ever be short-term.

People who are under entitled leaders will never be able to build the kind of meaningful connections that can grow a family or organization. Growth can only happen when people feel safe and respected, and that is only possible when they see that their leaders are willing to serve in the same way they are asked to serve.

So what did I do to course correct, and how did Jesus' actions inspire me to change? Let's find out.

The People I Work For

In my season of selective service, I emotionally damaged my kids and my wife by neglecting those relationships. At some point, I realized the bad choices I was making and wanted to transform the way I showed up at home. This led me back to Jesus to see what He did when He wanted to serve those He loved.

The real love of Jesus Christ was totally sacrificial. We see that in the example where He washes the disciples' feet. But further than that, His service and sacrifice is shown to be infinitely stronger when we see Jesus on the cross—dying to save humanity from our sins.

While we are not tasked with the salvation of humanity like Jesus was, each and every day, we are faced with opportunities to carry our own mini-crosses (which we'll talk more about in chapter 11). We can choose to carry these mini-crosses when we serve and sacrifice for the people we work with and live with.

At work, I had already figured out a system for this. I would teach my team members that any type of task or thing that they did for others was also serving them because of the way they would grow through service. This was a clear path to a mutually beneficial relationship, which is the fruit of service and causes lasting happiness and fulfillment.

In the case of Jesus, His dying on the cross benefited Him and God as Jesus' sacrifice created a path to a relationship with us— those whom God loves. But the main benefit was to us; through this action, humanity was saved from the consequences of our sins.

In the office I would explain to those around me that service is our way to happiness, but in order to understand service, we have to know what real love is. What Jesus taught is a sacrificial love. Not the kind of love we see in society today, which says, "I will love you until that becomes inconvenient and you no longer give me what I want or need."

When I sat down to mentally work through what I was doing at home, I came to a conclusion that grieved my heart: I had not given my family unconditional love.

When Jesus models this kind of love for us, the "love" in "I love you" is a verb: an action word. It means that you choose—every moment of every day—to love that other person.

During this season at home, I wasn't choosing to actively love my family. I wasn't actively loving my wife or supporting her. I wasn't sacrificing for her or serving her. And I wasn't doing those things for my children either.

As I started to think about how to change the situation at home, I couldn't help but think back to my wedding to Scarlett and the vows I made. In a Catholic wedding ceremony, the priest never asks you how you feel. The priest doesn't ask the groom, "Do you love your bride?" Instead, he asks, "Are you *willing* to love this person? Are you ready to *give your life* for this person?"

Marriage is a commitment and an act of will. It's not up to your feelings.

Scarlett and I met at a dental practice in Florida. She was a patient coordinator and I was a dental assistant. We started our business together ten years later.

For better or worse sounds great, but what they are really asking in that part of the ceremony is, "If this person goes through physical or emotional difficulties, are you going to love them or are you going to quit on them?" The answer cannot be about your *feelings* if love is a choice.

Love means you are choosing to sacrifice, so when you say, "I love you," it really means, "I sacrifice myself for you. I give myself to you."

As I started to compare the way I treated those I worked with to the way I treated my family, I saw there was a glaring difference. At work, I had always said, "These are the people I work for," when I talked about my team. And once I realized what was going on in my personal life, I wanted to be able to say, "These are the people I work for," about my family too.

In order to make that goal a reality, I knew some big changes needed to happen. That's when I decided to get disciplined about my time in a purposeful way so that I could show up even more for my family as a servant leader.

A regimented schedule allowed me to be there for my wife, my kids, and myself in a more productive way. Watching fútbol games with a beer in my hand became a thing of the past.

It was only when I was willing to make this change that I finally started to feel happy. Why? Here's an example that has always stuck in my head when I think about what it means to finally get what you want. And as you're about to see, I can relate strongly to the dog in this situation.

A Dog with a Metal Rabbit

If you've ever watched greyhounds race around a track, you know that they don't run for the fun of it. They actively chase what they think is a rabbit. One of the attendees at the race course will bring out the "rabbit" and show it to all of the dogs before the race. Then, once the race begins, the dogs go after it with great stride and purpose. With a clear goal, they launch themselves leap by leap in an attempt to catch what they think is their prey. But there is an illusion involved in this process.

The dogs think that if they run as fast as they can, they will be able to catch the rabbit at some point, but this isn't true. The metal rabbit was created with the specific purpose of keeping the dogs running race after race.

Did you know, though, that if they ever catch the "rabbit," take a bite of it, discover it is made of metal instead of flesh and bones, that they will lose all of their motivation to chase it forever? The dog that catches the "rabbit" will never race again.[9]

And this is exactly how I felt when I finally "achieved" all of the financial goals I had set for myself. Let me explain.

This is what it is like for us when we go after *things* in life: money, houses, cars, businesses, etc. Sometimes, we are trying to reach goals that are based on doing good only for ourselves, and then we get what we've been working toward—something we've been chasing our entire lives. But when we get whatever it is, we realize that what we wanted isn't what we thought it would be, and our world crumbles.

We feel empty inside. We lose *all* of our motivation. Just like the dog that catches the rabbit. When they realize that the trophy they wanted won't satisfy them, there is a mental switch that flips to "off." They will never chase the metal rabbit again since they know the promise of the rabbit is a lie.

But this doesn't happen to us when we invest in building and growing the relationships that matter deeply to us. And these relationships exist both at home and at work. Why don't we lose our motivation when we serve the people we have these relationships with? That's an important question to consider.

---

9   J.D. Greear, "A Powerful Lesson from Greyhound Racing," *Outreach Magazine*, September 23, 2019, https://outreachmagazine.com/features/discipleship/47110-a-powerful-lesson-from-greyhound-racing.html.

Sacrifice Means Love—Love Means Happiness

One of the things that has changed my life the most was becoming a father. Once I realized I needed to leave my selective service days behind me, days based on serving myself based on growing my own comfort, something amazing happened. As I reflected on God's unconditional love for me, I became more aware of needing to show that same unconditional love to my children.

There is this moment when you hold your baby for the first time. Every parent knows what I'm talking about. A little, wiggling miracle of a human looks up at you, and the world transforms instantly. You think, *No one will ever harm this baby because I would die before I let that happen!* But your baby doesn't know about your love for them yet. And there is no way they can love you back. Somehow though, even as the weeks progress and your baby keeps you up all night, you still feel this unconditional love for them. You think, *I don't care how many times you spit up on me, you are still the most amazing person I've ever met.* This is a selfless love, where you get nothing back. But you are still showing up hour after hour to serve that child and to sacrifice your own comfort for them.

This is the most beautiful example of what real love is. And this is how we are supposed to love everyone.

When I look at my wife, I need to choose to love her unconditionally, no matter what is going on. Even when she's mad at me (and probably for good reasons). Even when I don't *feel* like loving her.

In the professional space, this is also how we need to look at the people we have been entrusted to lead. We need to love them unconditionally and serve them. We need to sacrifice for them in a way that costs us.

Because it is only when we serve and sacrifice for others that we experience real happiness and true fulfillment. Now, what does this look like in the professional world? And how can this approach impact your team?

The Sacrificial Servant Leader

As you embrace these principles and work to become a sacrificial servant leader, there are two big questions that I want you to think about. First, what do you have to be willing to do in order to become this type of leader? And second, what kind of impact does this type of leader have on the people around them?

By taking a look at the answers to both of these questions, you'll be able to understand how to make sacrifices to serve those you lead. And this can change the world around you one person at a time—an idea we talked about in chapter 8 that we are going to dive deeper into here.

What Do You Need to Be Willing to Do?

In order to serve and sacrifice for others, the first step is to think about the people around you as the people that *you* work for. This style of leadership doesn't work if you think about your team as working for you.

Everything you do has to be in service of helping those around you grow into their gifts while supporting their goals.

As I look at my team, I have learned to ask myself, "What do they need in order to succeed?" and "What can I give them in order to help them accomplish what they are doing for our organization according to their gifts?"

The leader of an organization really needs to be the most sacrificial person on the team. And the same is true for your family.

If you can't sacrifice, you can't lead.

This means that in order to see the people around me succeed, I need to put their needs first.

We've talked about this previously, but I think it's worth mentioning here again: Loving others doesn't mean devaluing yourself. Sacrifice is supposed to cost us, yes. But it shouldn't damage us in a way that keeps us from being able to live healthy and balanced lives. When we're sacrificing for others because we want their love and approval, that is not unconditional love.

The foundational piece for being able to sacrifice for others and therefore love them needs to come from God. We see this after Jesus washes the disciples' feet when He says:

> A new commandment I give to you, that you love one another; even as I have loved you, that you also love one another.
> –John 13:34

Part of choosing to act based on love is also related to understanding that God loves us and that He has made each one of us unique.

Here's a simple example: When a patient walks into one of our dental clinics, we really need to mean it when we ask, "How can I help you?" Under these words, we have to say to ourselves, "I care so much about this one person in front of me. They are unique and amazing, and they chose to spend time with me. What can I do to help them with what they need at this moment?"

There is so much indifference in the world, and that feeling of "I don't really care" is destructive to the relationships we have and the ones we are building. It is also true that when we focus on ourselves, that selfish feeling we get is indifferent to what others need or want. This is another way that indifference is damaging to our relationships.

Sometimes in service, we see that team members are focused only on their own problems or drama. They might think, *I don't have time to deal with anyone else's problems because I have enough of my own.* But this thought is dangerous to someone who wants to become a sacrificial servant leader. This kind of thought can become a mentality that will keep you from really wanting to serve others. When you let feelings that come from entitlement keep you from acting, which we talked about earlier, that is when you are in real danger of not transforming into a servant leader.

Now, let's get into what kind of impact you can have when you embrace service and sacrifice as a leader.

The Impact of a Sacrificial Servant Leader

You already know that I am a huge fan of St. Teresa of Calcutta. But what you don't know is that I went to meet some of her nuns in the poorest area of Lima, Peru. Normally, this wouldn't be a place that someone would go because it's not safe. When I was there, I saw those nuns living lives that are completely opposite of what the world says will make them happy. They are ministering to others and praying for them all day, every day. Serving others.

As I met them in person, something impacted me that I will remember for the rest of my life. These nuns were the happiest people I've ever met. I could literally sense joy radiating from them. And as I watched the way they behaved and spoke, I realized that a lot of this joy was from their consecration— being set apart to live out a vow based on their radical love for Jesus.

I wanted to be close to them. I wanted to follow them. I wanted to become like them.

This is what will happen to you when you become a sacrificial servant leader too. People will want to be around you. They will follow you. They will want to become like you. Why?

When you are a leader who is willing to serve and sacrifice for someone else, you become more of an impactful leader to them. You become attractive to them because love is attractive.

Whatever message you have, it will become more impactful when you love others sacrificially.

And if you feel overwhelmed thinking about how many people there are on your team who need this type of service-based leadership, don't worry. All you have to do is start with one person. Decide that you are going to sacrifice for them specifically and that you are going to allow yourself to incur a cost to help them. You will be amazed by what will happen next, as this creates a ripple effect that has the potential to reach every corner of your organization.

When you think about your family, imagine what this kind of leadership—based on service and sacrifice inspired by unconditional love—can do to totally transform the lives of the people you love most. And as you'll see in the next few chapters, it was embracing leadership based on sacrifice and service that finally turned things around for the relationships I had within my own family.

Summary

- Jesus is the ultimate example of a servant leader.
- Service and sacrifice are qualities that can spread through your home and organization if they are modeled by servant leadership.
- Trying to lead by entitlement doesn't work long-term because it isn't inspiring.
- I work for the people in my organization, not the other way around.
- I need to work for my family in the same way with unconditional love and sacrifice.
- Often, when we get what we really want in life that's related to material wealth, we end up feeling empty and lose motivation—like the dog with the fake metal rabbit.
- Sacrifice means love—love means happiness.

- We need to be willing to care for others and to want to help them in a sacrificial way that fights against indifference.
- Sacrificial leadership from us will inspire others to follow up and provide service and support to others.

Actions to Take

A Service and Sacrifice Survey

As you process the thoughts and concepts I shared in this chapter, there is a collection of tools I want to teach you about. They make up some of the most important resources in your life: the people around you. Think about someone you trust who has encouraged you in the past. Then ask them if they'll help you with the following assignment.

Go through the questions below with them to get a clear picture of where you are as far as service and sacrifice and where you want to be as you improve your skills in these leadership areas.

1. Do I naturally look at the people around me and think about how I can serve them?
2. When I notice that someone needs help, do I ever seem indifferent to their situation?
3. Is there someone in my family that you think I could invest in sacrificing more for? If yes, who?
4. Is there a person I talk about at work that I could serve better as a leader? If yes, who? If not, can we think of a few people together that I could focus on serving?
5. Are the things I'm focused on achieving in life based on improving my relationships by serving others? If no,

how can I reduce my material goals so that I can focus on more relational ones?

For each question where you answered "yes," you're on the right track. For those you answered "no" to, brainstorm with the person you picked to go through these questions with. Create a plan for how you can improve your abilities to serve and sacrifice in the future.

Chapter 10

HUMILITY—THE MOST IMPORTANT MARK

Your leadership becomes more impactful when you are humble, because the humble person sees and accepts their own limitations as opportunities for growth.
—A Dr. Dan One-Liner

Throughout these pages, we have looked at 6 different marks of leadership. At the beginning of the book, I shared with you that humility is the most important mark, and that's the reason I wanted to save it for last. In this chapter, we are going to look at what humility means and why I call it the king of all virtues.

When I talk about humility in front of my team members or an audience at a speaking engagement where I'm serving leaders, I always think about a saying by St. Bernard of Clairvaux. This saint was a talented writer who battled with lifelong illness that inspired his intense closeness with God, while at the same time, he worked to establish an abbey in Clairvaux, France.[10] When he was asked what the Cardinal Virtues are, he responded:

"Humility, humility, humility, and humility."[11]

With that advice in mind, it is important for us to dig deeper and ask: What is humility, really? And are there things that show up looking like humility that really have nothing to do with being humble? Let's find out.

Another one-liner my team frequently hears me say is, "A humble person is an instrument of unity." And that unity coming from someone who is humble can help everyone around them establish a high-level view of humility by their example. Humility is the only mark of leadership that builds unity in such a powerful way. What do I mean?

Humility means that we view every person as valuable, without seeing ourselves as more important than anyone else.

We've already talked about how in order to love ourselves, we must acknowledge that God made each one of us as a unique bundle of cells who has certain gifts that help us work to serve others. It is good and right to say, "I am an amazing person full of talents." Beyond believing that, we can also inspire others with the gifts and talents we have.

The danger comes when we say, "My gifts and talents make me *more* valuable or important than anyone else."

---

10   John Richard Meyer, "St. Bernard of Clairvaux," *Encyclopædia Britannica*, March 11, 2025, https://www.britannica.com/biography/Saint-Bernard-of-Clairvaux.

11   Marcellino D'Ambrosio, "Sunday Reflection—Humility Opens Doors," *Integrated Catholic Life*™, August 31, 2019, https://integratedcatholiclife.org/2019/08/dambrosio-sunday-reflection-humility-opens-doors/.

Humility is knowing that you are valuable but still not more important than other people—especially those you serve in your leadership role. This is the part of humility that begins to builds unity. And humility also works to unite us by bringing us to a place of acknowledgement that we are all valuable, and collectively, our value multiplies when we are together. This is why humility is the king of all virtues.

However, we also need to be aware of something I call false humility, which I would say is negative. A lot of people might define this as someone who is only pretending to be humble while they are actually engaging in pride (which we will talk about later as I share my own story of how destructive pride can be).

Instead of defining false humility by its common definition, engaging in pride, I would define false humility as what happens when someone takes a low view of their own value. In practical terms, false humility exists when someone won't take credit for the things they do out of love and with their gifts to bring value to others. They want to keep a low view of themselves so they refuse to acknowledge the loving ways they have behaved toward others.

If you can't accept a compliment when it is relevant to what you've been doing to try to make the world a better place, you aren't valuing yourself: This is false humility.

For example, if you tell me, "Daniel, it is amazing that you've been able to create a team that supports each other based on how they love one another," and I say, "Oh, that's not really me. I can't take credit for that," then I am engaging in false humility.

But if I were to say, "Thank you. I am blessed to pass on to others what God has taught me," that is real humility.

When I'm talking about this concept with my team, I also point to a difference between importance and value. While these words sound similar in definition, when I'm speaking about humility, I think they offer a helpful distinction. Real humility is saying, "I know that I have personal *value*, but when I look at how *important* I am, I realize that everyone is equally important."

Importance is when you compare yourself to those around you to establish some kind of order. A lot of times, this temptation comes when you look at your organization chart and see who is toward the top. Maybe you see managers as more important than team members, or, as the CEO, you have been taught to think you are the most important person in the room. Humility compels us *not* to view people as more or less important than one another.

On the other side of importance is value. Value teaches us to look at each individual person and understand that their specific gifts are just as unique and valuable as the gifts of anyone else on the team—including the managers and CEO. There is often a tendency for humans to organize our thoughts about others based on the importance we associate with them, which is magnified in the business world. Why? Because when we accomplish so many things, we might think we are doing all of the important (there's that word again) tasks on our own, which brings us a lot of praise because of the way our society prioritizes importance.

So when you look at yourself, the distinction between importance and value is crucial. Yes, you are valuable, just as valuable as anyone else. But humility teaches that you are not more *important* than anyone else.

Similarly, at home, you might be tempted to look at your family structure like you would an organization chart and think, *Both of the parents are at the top, and the kids are underneath, so they are less important.* But when you look at your spouse and kids through the lens of humility, you can acknowledge freely that everyone in your family is equally as valuable. This means that you don't allow your own desires (what you want most) to dictate everything that happens in the home.

The presence of each unique, valuable individual in your family means that you have to make decisions based on the value of each member. You have to take a collective survey of what each person needs and then come to a decision that is based on what is good for everyone, not just what one person wants—and especially not just what *you* want.

I know how damaging the tendency to make choices for your family based solely on your own desires can be. Even though I was doing well at work, I was failing at home. And my lack of humility played a huge part. Remember how my entitled thinking helped me justify my choices at home where I would ignore my family so that I could sit alone with my beer to watch fútbol? The only person I was valuing in that decision was myself. That was pride at work in my heart.

When we don't have humility, we're embracing something different—prideful self-concern. You see, the way we view ourselves on the imagined organization chart that tells us we're more important than others is giving in to the sin of pride, and that's exactly the sin that became my downfall at home.

But it wasn't until I really started looking for inspiration in the lives of Jesus and the saints of the Church that I realized how important humility is.

Humility in Action

The Life of Jesus

When we look at the life of Christ, we can see how sacrificial His mission was. He cherished every person He encountered during His ministry on Earth. Jesus also treasures each one of us so deeply that He surrendered to the Father's plan to die on the cross. We can see exactly what His humility looked like in action when we read the following verse:

> Have among yourselves, which is yours in Christ Jesus, who, though he was in the form of God, did not count equality with God a thing to be grasped, but emptied himself, taking the form of a servant, being born in the likeness of men. And being found in human form he humbled himself and became obedient unto death, even death on a cross.
>
> –Philippians 2:5-8

And we can also look at some of the words that came from Jesus Himself:

> Take my yoke upon you, and learn from me; for I am gentle and lowly in heart, and you will find rest for your souls.
>
> –Matthew 11:29

When you are "lowly in heart," this means that you don't see yourself as more important than others. This is not the same thing as refusing to acknowledge the value God has given you. Jesus was lowly in heart, and He was willing to sacrifice everything to take the consequences of our sins. At the same time, He didn't deny His power or deity (His divine nature and status).

When we walk humbly with God (which is what we see God telling us to do in Micah 6:8), this means we understand the value He has placed on others and our unique selves by loving us into existence. At the same time, this means we understand we are all the same in importance.

Even if you don't believe in Jesus as the Son of God, you can still acknowledge that historically, He was a humble leader. He didn't wield His power against others. He invited others to come to Him in a way that showed the people He interacted with how valuable they were—based on His focused love for each unique individual. And we can see this by looking at the impact Jesus has had on others through the ages.

Historically, as we look at followers of Jesus, we see that they have also taken on the primary mark of leadership—humility. Someone who embodies this concept so well is St. Josephine Bakhita.

Not So "Fortunate" At First

Mother Josephine Bakhita was born into a loving family but was kidnapped into slavery in Sudan when she was 8 years old. Her captors gave her the name Bakhita, meaning "fortunate," as a joke because of her new situation.[12] And because of the horrific conditions she lived through, she forgot the name that had been given to her by her parents.

Eventually, after suffering extreme emotional and physical trauma as a slave, she was traded to the Italian Consul Callisto Legnani, who treated her with consideration and respect. When the Legnani family was forced to flee to Italy for political reasons, Bakhita asked for and was given permission to follow them.

Once in Italy, a friend of the Legnani family, the wife of Mr. Michieli, asked if Bakhita could stay with their family. So Bakhita went with the Michielis and when their daughter, Mimmina, was born, Bakhita became her caretaker.

When Mr. and Mrs. Michieli left to manage a hotel in Suakin on the Red Sea, due to the far distance and the difficulties of travel at the time, they entrusted Mimmina and Bakhita into the care of the Canossian Sisters at their Catechumen's Institute in Venice, Italy. And that is where Bakhita learned about God, and decided to devote her life to Him, embracing the virtue of humility fully.

After the Michielis came to get their daughter, Bakhita stayed with the sisters and went through the sacraments of Christian initiation. As her story came full circle, she was given the name Josephine, which means, "God will increase."

---

12   M. Shawn Copeland, "A Woman of Courage, Fortitude and Hope," *National Catholic Reporter*, February 24, 2010, https://www.ncronline.org/books/2022/06/woman-courage-fortitude-and-hope.

Mother Josephine Bakhita spent the rest of her life serving others in the freedom Italy granted her, instead of the slavery she began her life in. In Schio (located in Vincenza), the place she spent most of her life, the people there still call her "Our Black Mother."[13] It was through her humility in addressing the evil that had happened to her that she most influenced the lives of the people around her.

You can see the joy of Mother Josephine Bakhita in her eyes

According to the testimony of those around her, she was heard many times saying that, "If I were to meet the slave traders who kidnapped me and even those who tortured me, I would kneel

---

13   *Catholic Culture*, "St. Josephine Bakhita Was a Humble Witness to God's Love," accessed April 8, 2025, https://www.catholicculture.org/culture/library/view.cfm?id=3158.

and kiss their hands, for if that did not happen, I would not be a Christian and Religious today."[14]

Now she is known as the saint of internal freedom (meaning that inside, her thoughts and mindset were free to worship God in joy, despite her circumstances), and that was a liberty she treated with great humility. I only hope to be able to live with a tiny portion of the humility Mother Josephine Bakhita showed in the face of true evil in this world.

As I talk about Jesus and St. Josephine Bakhita, I can't help but think of this gem of wisdom from The Old Testament (which I can definitely relate to):

> When pride comes, then comes disgrace; but with the humble is wisdom.
>
> –Proverbs 11:2

I myself have lived the difference between pride and humility, so I know firsthand how difficult making choices based on humility instead of pride can be. In the next story, I'm putting my heart on the line. This isn't something that is easy for me to share, but the lessons I learned from going through such profound heartbreak (that was caused by my actions) are too valuable to keep to myself.

When My Sons Said Goodbye

As soon as my two oldest sons were old enough, they moved out. And it wasn't because I had taught them to be independent

---

14   *Catholic Mom*, "Responding to Evil with St. Josephine Bakhita," February 3, 2014, https://www.catholicmom.com/articles/2014/02/03/responding-to-evil-with-st-josephine-bakhita.

or to live in a way that honored each one of their unique values and gifts—the truth is that they wanted to be able to make their own decisions. At the same time, I felt like they didn't think they could trust me with what those desires were.

What my children absolutely needed from their father was for me to support their dreams and teach them what it means to become adults. And my sons also needed me to show them what it really means to be men who were willing to love and serve others. Unfortunately, I was too busy focusing on my own importance during this time to pay attention to what they needed.

In the last chapter, I shared that when I got home after working long hours at the office, all I wanted was a beer and to watch fútbol. From my perspective, I did the important work of earning the money for our family to live, and that let me off the hook for actually making sure to parent my children—I left all of that work to Scarlett. And while she did an amazing job, she could see our kids were suffering because of my lack of interest in their lives.

There were so many moments where she tried to help me see the truth, but I couldn't. I was blinded by my pride. I thought I was more important than my wife and kids. And it took something extreme to help me face my ugly, destructive sin.

At the time, when I looked at my life, I thought I was the perfect person. I had an outward image of success in all aspects of my life: My family looked amazing and loving from the outside, and we were involved in our church and community in a productive way. At least, that's what people saw until everything fell apart.

When my first son graduated from high school, he went to a super prestigious Catholic University. He is such a smart man, and during his senior year, he did an amazing job preparing and presenting a speech to more than 1,000 people.

Soon though, the cracks that existed from the lacking relationship I had with my son began to show. Within a year, he had dropped out of school and moved in with his girlfriend. Everyone in our local Catholic parish (the people in our community are part of the Church) found out, and even though there wasn't any judgment from those in my community, I was afraid of being judged by the people I encountered. That was my biggest concern at the time—my own reputation.

I was upset about the situation because of my own selfish reasons. When I look back, I think that might be why my son cut off communication with me—my behavior made him think that he had disappointed me. He didn't have any anger toward the rest of the family or any bad blood, but my self-concerned view probably discouraged him from staying in touch with us.

That's when I finally woke up to reality: I knew I had failed him. I was heartbroken, and I didn't know what to do to help us heal our relationship.

Then, my second son left for college. He wouldn't take any of my advice, and he certainly didn't want any of my money to help him make that transition. Our communication broke down soon after he left. It felt like our entire family was crumbling down, and it was all my fault.

I started to think back to all of the moments through the years when Scarlett had asked me to connect with the kids. Even with as much as she did, she was their mother—she couldn't also be their father. That was my responsibility.

When I looked back at my childhood, I thought I had an excuse. I would say to myself, "Well, my father didn't put a ton of effort into our relationship, and I turned out great." But that wasn't true. I wasn't living a humble life, and that hurt my wife and my children.

As I faced the hard truth, I realized I needed to acknowledge what I had done to help my family heal. At this time, I was an extremely prideful person. As hard as I had worked to keep that from the people at my Church, in my business, and even from myself, I needed to take responsibility for my own actions. It was time to stop hiding from the prideful person I had become.

Around this same time, I joined a group focused on helping men train their minds and their bodies. In terms of training my body, I lost 50 pounds in a few months. And I did the work I needed to do to train my mind so that I could face what I had done to my sons when I had neglected them.

So, when I went to confess my deficiencies to the boys, they were surprised, not just by the words I said, but by the way I looked. They could physically see that I was taking being disciplined in my life seriously.

I told each one of them, "I am sorry for not being more present in your life. The communication problems we have are all my fault. I want to support you and love you. I want to be the father you need. My pride blinded me, and I apologize. You are an amazing and unique gift to me, and I promise that is how I am going to treat our relationship from now on."

Today I am the joy-filled grandparent of two amazing grandsons. And even though I know the effort to maintain strong relationships is a continual journey that I need to prioritize, I now work with both of my sons in different businesses. Plus, we talk all the time, and I am an active force of encouragement and support for them because I make the time to be. My family members are the greatest blessings in my life.

I now know that my sons are just as valuable as I am. Humility taught me that.

I learned that as a leader in my house, I must treat my family with love and reverence. God entrusted these people to me, and that means I owe it to them to sacrifice for them, like Jesus sacrificed His life for me.

It took me seeing the pain my children were experiencing, because of what was going on in our family, to help me finally realize how destructive my pride was (and can still be if I don't embrace humility on a daily basis). I am so thankful for that wakeup call, because it allowed me to become a servant leader in my family as a sacrificial father.

This same sacrificial leadership, based on the power of true humility, is what can turn you into the kind of leader that will inspire people to support your vision and mission (which we talked about in chapter 2). With that in mind, now we'll take a look at the direct impact humility has on leadership.

Humility in Practice

The world will tell us that real leadership means we have to be outspoken about who we are and all of the accomplishments we've had. The world says that if we want to be taken seriously, that is—if we want to be respected—we need to act from an attitude based on the power we can wield. But in my business and in my family, I have found that the opposite is true.

And at the same time, I believe we can easily shift into false humility if we don't understand the following concepts.

When *you* are praised by someone, it is good to remember that you were made by God. And if someone is praising what you've done, they are also praising God. When this appreciation goes in the other direction, when you praise *someone* who was made by God, you are praising God.

Being a leader means that you acknowledge the others who are doing great things for you and in your life. This also means you are willing to receive compliments, like you feel comfortable giving out compliments. When you acknowledge the value you have by thanking others for noticing, you are still *embracing humility*. How?

If you believe in God, this means you look to Him as the author of who you are, and all of that belongs to Him. By recognizing His work and the great things He has given to you and entrusted you with, you are praising Him.

If you don't believe in God, you can still see and admit that the circumstances and resources you've been given in life have helped you get to where you are. These assets have helped you learn and given you precious moments of opportunity.

Taking a survey of our lives should reveal the events and situations that happened at the right time, in the right circumstances, and this bigger picture of how we've lived should keep us in humble positions.

Think about my life. I believe that God put my teacher Mr. Serra where he was at that time to help me. He was in my path during a time when I struggled in school, and he saw potential in me when I couldn't see it in myself. Even if you don't believe in God, you can see how much Mr. Serra did to change not only my life but the lives of those in my family and in my business.

It's why I don't believe that I am self-made.

I don't believe any self-made person exists.

In life, there are moments and opportunities that come together to create synchronicity, meaning that even when things seem unconnected, they can work together to connect for our benefit in specific ways.

The idea of synchronicity—circumstances working to help us—should shape our lives in ways that call us to embrace humility: We are valuable, yes, but no more important than anyone else.

When we lead with this thought, we will be able to equip and inspire those around us to each reach their full potential. When we lead from a place of putting ourselves at the top of the organization chart, refusing to value others, and thinking that our importance is what has given us what we need to succeed—that's when our leadership will fall short. It's that type of leadership that threatened to destroy my family. And it's that style of leadership that can take apart any seemingly successful business venture.

Humility gives us many opportunities to see our own limitations so that we can address them to leverage these opportunities to help others. This specific mark of leadership also helps us acknowledge the fact that we will always have room to grow, but that growth can only happen if we surround ourselves with others to support those efforts. Opportunities that are highlighted by limitations and community-supported growth are both huge advantages to any leader who wants to make a real difference in the world—and they are provided by true humility.

Now that you have worked your way through all of the 7 marks of leadership, it's time to see how they function together in 3 specific ways to support effective leadership in part 2 of the book. But first, let's close out this chapter and part 1 with the summary and actions to take.

Summary

- Humility means that we view every person as valuable and not see ourselves as more important than others.
- When we work together with humility as a common mark of leadership, it increases our unity.
- When we define our importance by treating life like an organization chart, we will feel tempted to prioritize our own importance.
- Jesus' humility is apparent when we look at His example on the cross.

- St. Josephine Bakhita demonstrated humility in the face of some of the deepest evil anyone can experience in this world.

- When I tried to lead my family by prioritizing my own importance, everything around me crumbled.

- It was only through facing my pride that I was able to heal the most important relationships in my life and become the leader my family needed.

- Synchronicity works for the benefit of each of us, meaning none of us is really self-made. Humility helps us embrace and leverage this fact.

Actions to Take

As you think about the way humility is currently showing up in your life, take the time to journal through the following questions.

- How are my current relationships at home shaped by my personal humility? Am I approaching my family as if we are all valuable, or am I putting myself higher than anyone else in terms of importance?

- At work, am I leading from a place of humility, or am I trying to do everything myself and work by insisting that I don't need help? Am I choosing pride?

- Can I take a compliment, or am I tempted to give into false humility that tells me I'm *not* valuable?

- Do I accept that failure is a part of life and that humility helps me see where I need the gifts of others?

Pride vs. Humility—Check-In Assessment

Answer the following questions with "Yes" or "No" as you go through them. Then read the text after the answers to understand how your answers can shape your updated approaches to humility.

1. Do you see each and every person you lead as being as valuable as yourself?
2. Are you able to work well with others in unity, allowing them to sometimes take the lead?
3. When you make a mistake, do you feel empowered to humbly ask for the help of someone else who has gifts in that related area?
4. Have you observed synchronicity (events that conspire in your favor) in your life in moments of success or triumph?
5. If you have difficulties at home, are you curious about what you could do differently?

If you answered "yes" to any question, you are on the right track. If you want to, make notes in your journal about how you can increase your humility in each of those situations and celebrate the way you've been aware of the value that each person has in context to the related question.

If you answered "no" to any of the questions, reflect on how you think of your importance in that situation. Then journal about areas of pride you recognize and how you can address them to shift your approach to be based on humility.

Part 2

LEADING PRACTICALLY WITH THE 7 MARKS

Chapter 11

TRAINED IN BEING
UNCOMFORTABLE

If you can't suffer, you can't lead.
–A Dr. Dan One-Liner

In this world, we will suffer. There is no getting around it. We have pain, we experience the horrific loss of death, and we see injustice all around us. In exchange, the world offers us something that we often believe can combat this suffering: comfort.

Pope Benedict XVI said, "The world will offer you comfort, but you were not made for comfort, you were made for greatness."

As I look back on my own story and the financial limitations I experienced, comfort was what I wanted most. I felt that if I worked hard and supplied my family with the finances for us to live, in exchange I would receive constant peace. And when that didn't happen naturally, I demanded it.

Telling Myself the Wrong Story

Back then, I would lie to myself, saying, "I am working endless hours and I need to do nothing but rest at home to better my family," while in reality, I was doing it for myself.

There was this story I told myself every day: The things I had worked hard to accomplish gave me an opportunity to reach the level of comfort I wanted, which I deserved. Growing up with financial scarcity, my ultimate goal was to work hard so that I could enjoy life without having to worry.

But this wasn't the story that would serve my family. As you read in the previous chapter, the family connections I should have been building with my sons and my wife fell apart when I was living my own story, one that removed me from as much suffering as possible. And this meant that I couldn't lead my family the way I should have.

I made work my god. I was telling myself the wrong story about my life and what I really needed to focus on, not realizing how destructive that would be. I needed to prioritize my family over myself. The unfortunate truth is when I made comfort my ultimate goal, my children interrupted that comfort, and they became a source of irritation. The tasks I needed to do to help my wife and kids became bothersome to me. This meant I was willing to compromise everything important in my life for a false sense of peace.

Professionally, my dental group grew, and we started to acquire talented people. At the same time, I started to slack on my leadership responsibilities at work. I was delegating solely to create more opportunities for myself. Even though I was still teaching the 7 marks of leadership you're reading about in this book, I wasn't living them in any area of my life. This created an incomplete version of leadership: self-service leadership. This morphed into the entitled leadership that I warned you about in chapter 9.

When you lead the right way, teamwork can create an amazing environment. In chapter 8, we talked about how when you lead, you need to empower others, but that wasn't what I was doing at that point in my career. It was through my constant seeking of comfort that my leadership at work was being destroyed—like it had been at home. But I was indifferent to all of this, and I didn't want to take on more projects at work while I was prioritizing my comfort over the growth of my family and my business.

While I knew I needed to change, I didn't understand yet that I needed to become a person who embraced feelings of discomfort instead of comfort. Training in discomfort was the only thing that would help me face my problems—problems that made me feel extremely uncomfortable—in order to transform the issues that, up until that moment, I had tried to hold at a distance.

I didn't realize that I had been telling myself the wrong story until I found a group of men at a dental conference who train CEOs through fitness. This encounter completely transformed my life. Let me set the literal stage for you.

Training of the Mind

Every year I attended this same dental conference. But this particular year, the master of ceremonies (MC) came on stage looking like a completely different person. It took me a moment to recognize him. He had lost 50 to 60 pounds—it was so dramatic, I thought maybe he had had some kind of surgery.

During his speech, he thanked a company he said we could find out in the table area in the lobby. I thought, *Wow*, and knew, seeing his weight loss results, that I needed to talk to the people he had given credit to.

You see, at this point in my life, even though I wanted to experience comfort all of the time, I felt physically horrible. I had been trying to lose weight for months. I was 45 years old with hurting feet and an aching back, and I felt sleepy all day long. Before the conference, I had tried working with several physical trainers, but I had always fired them after a few days, thinking, *Why would I want to make myself suffer by exercising? I'm not athletic. This isn't for me.*

So after the MC's speech, I marched over to the table of the company that he had mentioned and asked them, "What is different about your organization? Why should I trust you when nothing else has worked for me so far?"

The representative of the company's response was, "Because we don't care about your body. We train your mind. If you're doing this for any selfish reason, you will fail. We are successful because we train people in suffering. We want people to understand that to lead, you have to suffer."

What I would learn later is that in order to train my mind to respond well to situations that felt difficult or chaotic, as a leader, I needed to embrace suffering instead of preferring comfort. Why? When you train for comfort, even the most simple demands of everyday life will feel frustrating to you as you work to lead others.

At the time, my response was, "Sign me up!" Even though I didn't necessarily know what I was signing up for, the concept of training in suffering was interesting to me, and I wanted to know more.

Unlocking the 7 Marks of Leadership

Even though I already knew about the 7 marks of leadership by the time I met these trainers, the concepts they taught me unlocked so much more power within the 7 marks.

I had never thought to train in discomfort, but with this idea, my message was finally complete. This is what God used to transform my mentality. Discomfort was the missing piece I needed to finally lead my family well and to become the leader my dental group needed.

When I first told my wife, Scarlett, what I was doing, she was understandably frustrated. She had been telling me the same things all along, and now I was paying a company to teach me those lessons. If only I had listened to her earlier.

As I started to train in discomfort, pushing myself physically and mentally through the intense exercise training and nutrition-based boot camps I had paid for, I was finally able to live out the 7 marks of leadership. After working out for hours each morning, I learned to focus on foods that would make me *feel* good physically instead of only tasting good. It was a form of discipline I really hadn't ever subjected myself to, and it was extremely difficult.

The first results I saw were at home, where I realized the problem all along had been me. I was trying to live a selfish life, not a sacrificial one. I hadn't been showing up as someone willing to die for my family. And I wasn't loving them the way I've mentioned in previous chapters—by demonstrating sacrificial love.

The next big results came when I finally lived what I was teaching at work by embracing discomfort.

Yes, I would talk to my team at work about sacrificial love, but I hadn't been willing to die to myself in order to serve my family. I hadn't been willing to actually be uncomfortable or to sacrifice for the people I was leading.

Once the training program I signed up for at that conference started, I would do even more than what they told me to. I would do five sets of reps instead of three. I would do two hours of cardio instead of one. Honestly, this was my way of punishing myself for believing a story that was all wrong, one that had encouraged me to neglect my family.

Every morning, I got up at 3:45 a.m. and did this brutal camp that they set up with instructions online, all while eating only 1,700 calories of a high-protein diet throughout the day.

I also started to uncover some unconscious stories I'd been telling myself that weren't true. Since I grew up with financial limitations, I told myself that I needed to earn money and trust by being excellent all the time. This meant that my value came from school and then work—not directly from God. And in my mind, there was nothing worth loving about me aside from my professional success.

This meant that I was extremely uncomfortable facing my imperfections, because I felt like if I wasn't in that perfect zone all the time, I wasn't worthy of love. At work, I could work harder to achieve my idea of perfection because I am great at business, specifically what I do with the dental group. I would often get praised by people there for the things I did. At home, though—that was a different story.

That's when I realized I wasn't valuing myself the same way God values me. In chapter 2, I spoke about how God created you and me as unique gifts to be opened. And at this point in my life, I hadn't been treating myself or my family that way. I wasn't using my gifts to serve them. I was afraid that I didn't have any gifts that would be useful to my family.

Even though I knew I loved my wife and kids in theory, at this point, I knew I was failing at home, and I didn't want to face it. Only when I was willing to sit in my discomfort with these feelings could I face the imperfections I struggled against in myself and how I interacted with my family. That is when I was finally ready to make active changes.

Every day of the exercise and nutrition program, I was denying myself. And by this point, I didn't want to eat only that high-protein diet. I wanted a brownie! But I used my abilities to study and learn (gifts Mr. Serra had given me back in high school) to become excellent at my new routine. I lost 50 pounds in 4.5 months. In essence, though, it was so much more than weight loss that happened: I created a whole different life for myself.

I stopped drinking. This meant no more beer and fútbol. And with all of the time I spent working to become a truly sacrificial leader at home, those fútbol games were the next things to go.

Today, I am in the best shape of my life. I have never looked this way, even when I was younger. But that isn't the goal. I'm not continuing to do the same level of training because I want to feel or look good; those are just natural results. Now, what you see on the outside of me physically is a reflection of the man inside—someone who is willing to train in discomfort to face his imperfections in order to change them.

I am now a disciplined man, a strong leader, and someone who is ready to die for my family. And when I work to lead my team, I am coming from that same perspective. I value every person I work with by being willing to experience discomfort to make our organization better.

Now, I am the first one to sign up to sacrifice for others.

This is why each one of us needs to train in discomfort, as we all have imperfections we will need to face in different situations—and facing those imperfections means we will have to sit in discomfort if we want to work through them. The truth is being a sacrificial leader requires us to become selfless, and part of that is facing our imperfections and the imperfections of others as we lead. And the way to team up with the discomfort that comes from facing those things can only be developed through discipline.

One of the most powerful things I learned through this experience is that if we are not willing to suffer, if we are not trained in discomfort, then when chaos arrives, we will only think about ourselves—not others.

And that is no way to lead.

So how can you train in discomfort to unlock the next level of power when leading with the 7 marks? Let's find out.

Learn to Expect Chaos

Earlier we talked about a story I was telling myself. One that wasn't true. The problem for humans is that we sometimes tell ourselves the wrong stories. We say, "Poor me," and in doing so, we set the wrong expectations. As you've read about my life in this book, you can see that in all of the places where I said, "Poor me," instead of embracing the value God has assigned to me and the challenges He allowed in my life, things went downhill quickly.

Instead of trying to create comfort for ourselves, we should be training for chaos. We should expect chaos; it is an inevitable part of what life brings. No one is exempt. So we enjoy our moments of peace while we train for the chaos that is coming next. That way, when chaos arrives again, we'll be prepared for it.

We often want chaos to stay out of our lives, but that is the wrong expectation.

For example, you need to do the dishes after dinner, but you might feel tired. That task can become huge if you're only thinking of yourself. You might think, *My day was so chaotic and I'm exhausted—and it seems like I'm the only one who ever does this chore with its own brand of chaos as I look at this intense pile of dirty dishes. That must mean no one cares about me.* You might take one look at the pile of food and plates and say, "I just can't do this right now." That's what I *used* to say.

Before I trained for chaos, I would have emotional breakdowns pretty often. Now, they don't happen.

I now expect there to be disruption in my day, but I'm more than okay with that. Now I'm thinking of others instead of only thinking, *poor me.*

This newfound energy allows me to sign up for way more projects. Yes, I might have a lot more chaos in my life, but I still have peace because I am prepared to go to war.

When I first began this training program—when they said to expect chaos—I kept thinking about the training that US Marines and other military members go through. I used to think to myself, *Why would anyone sign up to go through these extremes where people come up to your face and yell at you, where you get a cold bucket of ice water thrown on you at 3:00 in the morning, or where you're forced to go to the cold beach to do planks?* This far into the training, I now understand that they are training soldiers to face death. These men and women are training in discomfort so that they know what to do when chaos comes.

Soldiers have to face death, so they prepare for it. But the reality is that we all have to face death. And when we discipline ourselves to say no to a brownie, we can use that same skill to say no to lying, gossiping, becoming indifferent, or being mean.

I learned the hard way that when we seek only comfort, we can destroy our lives. Why? Because seeking comfort is the destroyer of our potential. It isn't until we are tested that we really know what we are made of and what we can accomplish. And we cannot be tested or have the opportunities to grow without embracing discomfort.

Leaders must solve problems and face difficult issues almost every day—that is part of our job requirement—whether we're at work or at home.

The ultimate example of what it looks like to be willing to train in discomfort for the benefit of others is the life of Jesus Christ.

Jesus and the Crucifix

When I think about discomfort and chaos, I can't help but think about Jesus and the cross. Without the cross, the suffering, the willingness to die for us, and the selfless sacrifice He made—Jesus' story would be incomplete.

St. Bernadette Soubirous said, "Why must we suffer? Because here below pure love cannot exist without suffering."[15] We see that in the life, death, and resurrection of Jesus. He suffered on our behalf to cleanse us from our sins, all so that we could be reconciled to God, who is holy.

None of us can really love others unless we are willing to sacrifice, and Jesus made the ultimate sacrifice.

---

15   *Catholic Digest*, "St. Bernadette Soubirous—Why Must We Suffer?", March 3, 2021, https://www.catholicdigest.com/from-the-magazine/quiet-moment/st-bernadette-soubirous-why-must-we-suffer/.

That doesn't always look like literally dying for others, which is what Jesus did. But we all have opportunities to have these mini-deaths and mini-crosses every day by dying to our own wants. True love cannot exist without suffering, because if you want to avoid suffering, you are not willing to sacrifice for the other person—that's not true love.

When you choose love, suffering is part of that decision. That is when you choose to have those moments of sacrifice, a mini-death, for the person you are showing love to.

These moments act as mini-crosses for us to bear. The thieves who walked next to Jesus, also condemned to be crucified, were also carrying crosses, but they weren't embracing them like Jesus was. He was choosing to die out of love. And when He fell under the weight of the heavy cross, He got back up again because of His motivation—us.

As Jesus hung on the cross between the two thieves, there was a different response from each of them. Jesus was willing to suffer. The first thief asked Jesus to save the three of them, clearly not understanding Jesus' purpose on the cross. The other thief saw Jesus as a leader and a savior, and he told the first thief to stop tempting Jesus, who was there not because of what He had done, like both of the criminals were. What happened to the second thief?

> And he said, "Jesus, remember me when you come into your kingdom." And he [Jesus] said to him, "Truly, I say to you, today you will be with me in Paradise."
> –Luke 23:42-43

The second thief was inspired by Jesus' sacrificial love—the willingness of Jesus to be in the midst of chaos and discomfort in order to save all of us.

When we train in discomfort and learn to expect chaos, that's when we can create the biggest impact in our leadership, both at work and at home.

One of the best ways we can help train for chaos is by building up the currency of confidence in our daily lives, which is what we're going to explore more in the next chapter.

Summary

- We can either have comfort or greatness, but not both.
- The stories that we tell ourselves determine how we think and lead.
- In order to be ready for chaos, we have to train for it in our minds.
- Training in discomfort unlocks a greater power when using the 7 marks of leadership.
- Jesus embraced chaos when He died a sacrificial death on the cross. We have many opportunities each day to carry our own mini-crosses and experience mini-deaths to ourselves.

Actions to Take

Embracing Mini-Deaths

The next time you encounter a moment of discomfort, there is a quick way to encourage yourself to take action. As we've discussed in this chapter, make sure you're telling yourself the true story—one that includes expecting chaos and embracing mini-deaths.

Let's look at an example. Say you have to make dinner and you've just had the most difficult day on Earth. You're exhausted, and you don't know how to convince your hand to lift the knife and start chopping vegetables. There are two different stories you can tell yourself.

The "Poor Me" Story

I look at the kitchen and I feel betrayed. It's been a long day, and all I want to do is lie down. Exhaustion is winning over hunger. But my family needs to eat.

In my head, I hear a voice telling a story:

I hate that I have to cook right now. Poor me, that I have to do this after such a hard day at work. I'm doing all these things by myself, and no one in my family even cares. I'm alone and unappreciated.

In contrast, you can tell yourself a very different story.

The Privilege Story

I can feel the weariness in my bones, but I have trained for discomfort, and that means I know how to get through this. I look at the meal prep list on the fridge and I start to pull out ingredients.

In my head, I hear a voice telling a story:

I get to do this because of the love I have for these people. Sitting around the table together to listen and share about the different ways the day went for each member of my family will help me remember what's important.

It's Your Choice

In the second story, what you're witnessing is a mini-death.

Either way, dinner needs to get made. But with the second stream of ideas, the privilege story, making dinner becomes an act of love.

The next time you encounter a difficult moment, when you have an opportunity to suffer a mini-death—a moment of suffering and sacrifice for someone you care about—make sure you tell yourself the right story. The one that's based on love.

Chapter 12

THE CURRENCY OF CONFIDENCE

Quitting is training for failure.
—A Dr. Dan One-Liner

Imagine every day, as you lead your family and your team members at work, each decision you make costs you a little something. When you show up and serve others, a resource gets used up—it's one that can easily be depleted but can thankfully be rebuilt. When it comes to effective leadership, I believe there is a key currency you spend each and every time you make a choice on behalf of others—one that has the potential to make your life and every interaction you have better: That currency is confidence.

When you are a leader, you need to have confidence that what you're doing is right for the people around you. And if you don't, your family, your professional team, and even that little voice in your head telling you whether you're doing the right thing, will have a hard time trusting you.

In the last chapter, we talked about training in discomfort. I hinted a bit at discipline (through the exercise and nutrition program I did). In this chapter, we are going to break down how you can use discipline and other tools to create a currency of confidence that you can spend throughout each day on those who you serve and lead.

Then, at the end of the chapter, you'll have a chance to create your own first training regimen based on developing more confidence. This will help you show up as the leader the people around you need—both with your family and the people inside your organization.

As leaders, we are called to make the world a better place. The only way we can do this is by first leading ourselves by building up confidence.

Discomfort, which we talked about in the last chapter, provides us with opportunities to use discipline—and discipline is the first tool I want to talk about when it comes to building the currency of confidence for ourselves.

The Two Types of Discipline

When I think about the meaning of discipline, I would say that each moment of discipline is an exercise in self-denial. There are two ways this can show up in your life.

Do Something You *Don't* Want to Do

First, you could choose to engage in a task that gives you the opportunity to do something that would otherwise make you feel uncomfortable or inadequate. For this first option, I wouldn't count it as discipline when you're doing something you love. For example, if push-ups are your favorite activity, doing 100 of them each day doesn't really count as discipline, even though it is good for your body to engage in this particular activity.

An action doesn't count as discipline unless it's something you *don't* want to do but *choose* to do, regardless of your desire to avoid it.

When we encourage ourselves by taking actions we don't actually want to take, which I would call the practice of self-denial, that is how we lead our own selves. As leaders, this is something we must do every day. It is indispensable for a leader to have practice in self-denial. And over time, self-denial builds consistent discipline.

This is why I said that if you like doing 100 push-ups, that's not really an area of discipline for you, because even if they are physically difficult to do, there is no self-denial involved. But, for example, if you love to eat and you decide to fast from food two days a week, that is true self-denial. That kind of practice will build discipline in your life.

And when you can manage to accomplish something that you *don't* want to do, you are proving to yourself that you can manage difficult things, both mentally and physically. This is the first way that you can use discipline to create the currency of confidence. I'm going to go more into detail about what this means later in the chapter, but the discipline of doing things that are mentally difficult for you teaches your mind, over time, that you are capable of accomplishing things even when they are hard.

Knowing you have this ability will help you lead others well. If you operate from a place of having enough currency of confidence to trust yourself, others will trust you as well.

Now, let's take a look at the second way that discipline can be encouraged in your life.

Avoid Something You *Want* to Do

Another way to use discipline is to limit an activity or habit that you love. For example, in the last chapter I told you that I wanted to eat brownies when I was in the exercise and nutrition boot camp. By deciding not to eat brownies—since I wanted to train in discomfort, feel healthier, and show up for the people in my life without experiencing the sugar highs and lows—I was able to prove to myself that I could do difficult things. This increased my currency of confidence.

You don't have to pick something huge to practice this. In the Catholic Church, we observe Lent, which is when the Church invites the faithful to engage in prayer, fasting, and almsgiving as a way to prepare spiritually for Easter. And when we feel the absence of being able to eat meat, it gives us an opportunity to remember to pray and focus on God during the time of year we celebrate what Jesus did for us on the cross.

Whether you're doing something you *don't* want to do or avoiding something you *want* to do, the root of discipline is cultivated by the concept of self-denial. It is this powerful idea that creates an opportunity to build the currency of confidence through discipline. So, why don't we take a closer look?

The Gift of Self-Denial

When we choose to act in self-denial, it gives us great practice at being uncomfortable—at training in discomfort.

I've already told you that I lost 50 pounds and completed an intense workout and nutrition boot camp in order to discipline my mind. To train in discomfort. But I still work out for 90 minutes every day. And if I'm honest, I still don't ever really enjoy it. This is a continuous way to train myself in discomfort, to prepare for the coming chaos life can deliver, seven days a week.

My commitment to doing 90 minutes of physical training is based on knowing that when I give my word to someone, that matters—even when the person I've given my word to is myself.

What we say we will do is important. If we commit to something, we have to stick to it, no matter what. This is where follow-through comes in. If you tell yourself that you're going to do an activity that you normally drag your feet to do, then you have to do it. Why? Because quitting is training for failure. And when you neglect to follow through on something you have promised to yourself, you are communicating to your own mind that you *are* a failure.

You have neglected to keep your word, even if no one else ever heard the promise you made.

And if you tell yourself that you are going to avoid doing something you love so that you can practice self-denial to build more of a currency of confidence. If you keep those promises to yourself, you are communicating to your brain that you are the kind of person and leader you say you are. You kept your word, and that builds your character (something we're going to touch on as a tool to create the currency of confidence).

Strong, confident leaders identify as disciplined individuals who are committed to doing what they say they will do. The battle inside your mind to do what you've said is one that you have to face every day. And the best way to build confidence over time is to keep your promises to yourself. A great way to practice this is to create intentional tasks that are based on self-denial.

Think about it this way: If you give yourself a task where you can practice discomfort based on self-denial, and you complete that task, you have achieved a victory! This is why I think of self-denial as a gift: It gives you a chance for a small win each time you choose it. That also happens each time you choose not to engage in an activity that you love so that you can focus on training in discomfort.

When you face battles every day, like getting up at 4:00 a.m. to work out (which I'm never personally excited about), and you complete that workout, you've won. You've faced a battle early in the morning and came out victorious. You have earned credits in the currency of confidence that you can use throughout the rest of your day. That sets you up to lead well for the entire day when you already had your regular session of training in discomfort and you came out triumphant.

LITTLE DAILY WINS LIKE THIS WILL HELP YOU PROVE TO YOURSELF THAT YOU CAN FOLLOW THROUGH ON YOUR PROMISES.

This builds the currency of confidence that is available to you so that you can continue to grow each and every day.

A new day is a new battle and another opportunity for you to get that little win. And what if you could capitalize on these types of wins by becoming part of the 1%?

The Confidence of the 1%

To continue to build currency of confidence for yourself over time, you need to choose to do something that is hard—an activity that not everyone would be willing to do.

Effective leaders need to work in ways that build more of the currency of confidence that will take them to a level where they can really serve others. They need to aim to become more than average—they must aim for excellence.

How can those of us who want to be amazing leaders at work and at home do that?

Let me give you an example. According to a video called "The One Thing Only 1% of People Do," by Jim Kwik, the most successful people don't have a to-do list. They have a don't-do-this list. A list of nonnegotiable things they won't engage in since it is impossible for any one of us to do everything.

The number one thing on the don't-do-this list is to check your phone first thing in the morning. Why? Because it changes your brain chemistry by giving you dopamine hits based on what you find on your phone instead of leaving your brain in its default creative morning mode that opens you up to having your best ideas.

Deciding not to check your phone first thing in the morning could become a planned action of self-denial. We all want to check our phones first thing in the morning, but this teaches our brains to engage in digital distraction (which refers to an interruption created by an electric device or online activity that disrupts one's focus and detracts attention away from a more meaningful or helpful activity).[16]

Would you be willing to do something that helps you instead of checking your phone? Maybe you choose to meditate first thing in the morning. For me, I prioritize doing my daily prayers, and then I do the 90-minute workout that I find personally challenging.

By replacing the action of checking your phone first thing, which is something everyone wants to do—you become part of the 1% who avoids this behavior. This decision gives you confidence in yourself by having a quick moment of victory early in the morning. And it also communicates to your brain that you are working to be more than average: You are pursuing excellence.

Then, you can build on that with a difficult, even more uncomfortable choice as you work to increase the currency of confidence in your life through discipline and self-denial—all while you aim for excellence.

---

16   Jim Kwik, "The One Thing Only 1% of People Do," *Motivation Madness*, YouTube video, February 3, 2020, 10:13, https://youtu.be/hz4NpIl0kYg.

We are all made for greatness, but training in discomfort. Practices like refusing to seek digital distraction first thing in the morning, and working to build confidence daily by using self-denial practices, is required for us to embrace and realize that greatness.

Negative Forces Fighting for You to Stay Average

The practices, like the ones I mentioned earlier in this chapter, are required of you as a leader. If you want to lead, you have to excel and be extraordinary.

One thing that is important to understand when you are working to build more of a currency of confidence is that there are negative forces fighting against you all the time—not to turn you into a failure but to keep you average. In Christianity, we consider Satan and those on his side to be negative spiritual forces. And in our world where things age and fall apart over time, another negative force we can point to is entropy, which breaks down physical excellence over time.

Why do these forces want to keep you average? Someone who is average doesn't impact others, and they certainly don't impact the world.

Like we talked about in chapter 2, you were loved into creation by God as an amazing and unique person, and when you give into those negative forces that want to make you average, you are departing from the reason that you were created. If you surrender to negative forces, that will absolutely impact your leadership potential. This is why you need the currency of confidence: This is the resource you can use to fight against these forces so that you can keep doing good in the world.

When I walk into a room feeling like I've built myself more currency in confidence by rejecting the negative forces that want to keep me average, my entire perspective shifts. I'm thinking, *It's only 10:00 a.m. and I've already conquered a lot of battles so far today.* My team senses that. They can feel it.

And by keeping your word to yourself, you can reject those negative forces—like temptation, comfort, or pride.

Going after excellence is a powerful tool for creating more confidence currency, but there is still another amazing tool we haven't discussed. And this tool is vital for developing as a servant leader in any area of your life.

Improving Our Character

When we work on increasing our currency of confidence every day, we will be much better prepared to face our own imperfections. How? Because when we practice using all of the tools (that we've gone through) each day, we will feel confidence in the face of discomfort. And this helps us realize the final tool I want to discuss in this chapter: improving our character.

The truth is that it is uncomfortable to face our failings and shortcomings—our imperfections. But this awareness is critical when the temptations we feel (like pride or entitlement) can present choices we know aren't good for us.

When I think of a choice that isn't good for me, I view it as a temptation. Confidence is necessary to fight against temptations. A temptation arises when you know there is a behavior that goes against your character, but you want to indulge in it anyway.

For example, let's say that you have access to funds in a business, and you're in a season of needing to pay off a few debts. Looking at the amount of money you have access to might make you think of how glorious it would be if you used the money that's not yours to increase your credit score to 750 and to pay off your debts. Then you could finally get a mortgage on the house of your dreams.

But if you took those funds, you would be going against your good character. That's embezzlement. You would be giving into the temptation to steal what is not yours. And you would be depleting your currency of confidence and communicating to yourself that you can't be trusted to make decisions that prove you have good character.

At home, this might look different. It could be that you really, really want to buy something expensive that you know your spouse won't support purchasing. Maybe it's a boat that you really won't ever use. You have friends who just bought boats, and now you want one too. So you go in secret to buy a boat and avoid telling your spouse about it. In this case, you have been tempted to covet (to want what someone else has), to deceive your spouse by not telling them what is going on, and then you continue to deceive them by keeping the boat purchase a secret.

Then, when your child suddenly needs a tuition check for the next semester of school, the money is no longer available, because it went toward your secret boat's down payment. Your lapse in character, your giving into temptation, put your family in a tricky position, and now your child might have to transfer schools.

In this case, you would again be depleting your currency of confidence; your actions are evidence to your mind that you can't be trusted. This shows a lack of the discipline or self-denial that demonstrate you are capable of being an excellent leader.

These are just examples, and while I highly doubt you would steal from your company or spend your child's tuition money on a boat, I want you to see that every choice we make comes back to character. And when we are confident that we can make decisions that train us in discomfort every day (through all of the tools we've listed that create the currency of confidence), that's when we will be able to stand against temptation. How?

Look back at the embezzlement example. If you are trained in discomfort, you can stay uncomfortable in your debt and make an ethical plan to pay off what you owe over time. You will be able to use financial actions that involve self-denial to save your money while maintaining your confidence and character.

Thinking about the boat situation, if you are confident in your abilities and disciplined enough to train in discomfort and tell yourself "no" often, then you can resist purchasing a boat. By thinking about the fact that you don't have to keep up with any of your friends by buying something you don't need, something you know your spouse wouldn't want, you can use your credits of currency in confidence. You are reminded that you win battles every day, and that speaks to your character and who you really are. Plus, you're prioritizing your child's education by sacrificing so that you can send them to a high-quality school.

And when you have good character, you will become a better leader because others will trust you. Your integrity will signal to them that they are safe in following your leadership and guidance.

Now that you have a baseline for understanding how confidence works, I want to move through the *different* tools of the currency of confidence and how they might show up as you experience areas of development—in order to be a leader who makes a difference in the world, you need to aim for excellence.

Opportunities for Development

Discipline, self-denial, and character development all play critical roles in every kind of journey you can imagine in life, especially when it comes to creating the currency of confidence.

As we think about these concepts and take them one step further, it is helpful to know that for each of us, there are both spiritual and physical benefits to flexing those confidence muscles.

Spiritual development happens when you work on your inner self—your soul, your thoughts, and your mindset. Physical development takes place when you focus on pushing past your limits in a healthy way to give yourself more physical strength and stamina. Both types of development will give you opportunities to build more currency in confidence, and they are more powerful when they are combined.

When you put in the time to practice self-denial to increase your spiritual knowledge and practices, that will build you up and refine your character (both of which create more confidence currency). And when you train your physical body through acts of self-denial or by doing things you *don't* want to do in the form of discipline (again, creating that currency), you will increase your confidence and build up your energy so that you are better able to serve and sacrifice for those around you.

Now, I want to zero in on the spiritual journeys we can take to encourage creating more confidence currency for ourselves.

In your spiritual development, it is important to be disciplined and practice with consistency to build habits that contribute to the continued development of good character in yourself. This is why I am so adamant about my daily prayer time.

And to take the spiritual side of development and discipline a step further, consider one of my favorite verses, Colossians 1:24, which teaches us, "Now, I rejoice in my sufferings for your sake, and in my flesh I complete what is lacking in Christ's afflictions for the sake of his body, that is the church."

When we suffer, whether it's spiritually or physically, we unite our sufferings with the sufferings of Christ.

This brings St. Padre Pio to mind. He created what is called the 5 Point Rule of Life and is most remembered for helping people deal with trying to live a holy life in the world (where negative forces want us to be average instead of amazing and unique).

These 5 points are: a weekly confession, a daily communion, an evening examination of conscience, a daily spiritual reading, and mental prayer twice daily.

About the fifth and final point, St. Padre Pio said,

> If you do not succeed in meditating well, do not give up doing your duty. If the distractions are numerous, do not be discouraged; do the meditation of patience, and you will still profit. Decide upon the length of your meditation, and do not leave your place before finishing, even if you have to be crucified. Why do you worry so much because you do not know how to meditate as you would like? Meditation is a means to attaining God, but it is not a goal in itself. Meditation aims at the love of God and neighbor. Love God with all your soul without reserve, and love your neighbor as yourself, and you will have accomplished half of your meditation.[17]

St. Padre Pio is encouraging discipline here. Spiritual discipline. He gives all of us five practical ways that will lead us into spiritual development, and now people all around the world know who he is because of how valuable this teaching was. These practices encourage communion with God, which leads us into consistency. And knowing God more means we understand Him better, and we understand His purposes for our lives better. This too builds more credits in the currency of confidence.

---

17 Sam Guzman, "St. Padre Pio's 5 Point Rule of Life," *The Catholic Gentleman*, August 21, 2014, https://catholicgentleman.com/2014/08/st-padre-pios-5-point-rule-life/.

You can see the peace on St. Padre Pio's face

The ministry of St. Padre Pio has been so impactful to the world and to my family that we actually went to see his body in the crypt of the Church of Our Lady of Grace in San Giovanni Rotondo, Italy, on our last family vacation. As a testimony to his ministry, his body has been preserved through the miracle of incorruptibility, meaning he has not experienced any decay.

But St. Padre Pio isn't the only example we have of how powerful spiritual development can be. Whether you want to lead at work or at home, following Jesus' example means that we have to unite ourselves with Him. And whether or not you follow Jesus, there are still unlimited benefits to be found from creating and acting on self-denial practices in your daily life— ones that may be similar to those suggested by St. Padre Pio.

One of the most important kinds of help that self-denial, discipline, and confidence create in our lives is something we already touched on a bit in the boat example: Validation, which I define as having external or internal recognition that your feelings make sense (or are valid). What does all of that mean? Time to find out.

The Validation to Conquer Your Desires

Validation happens for each of us when the feelings we have about the world and ourselves are confirmed. There are typically two types of validation that we seek: external and internal. External validation has to do with the way we interact with others. We want to be listened to, and we want to feel understood when others listen to us. But in this section, I want to focus more on what most people don't know they really need—internal validation—which is when you understand your own value (something we've touched on in multiple chapters, especially chapter 2).

If you are a young person starting your adult life, you're probably looking for massive amounts of external validation. That makes sense because you want to establish and understand your place in the world.

On the other hand, if you're older, you still want validation. Hopefully, by this point, you've found some as you traveled through your personal and professional life. You've realized that internal validation is actually more valuable than external validation. External validation tends to be more fleeting and inconsistent because it depends upon the behaviors of others. This is why it is so important for you to build the currency of confidence in yourself by using the four tools (and types of development) we've talked about in the book so far:

- The gift of discipline through self-denial
- Navigating forces that want to make us average by working to become excellent
- Developing good character
- Finding validation

No matter our age, we all still seek validation. We want to be understood. But many times, we don't consider whether we understand ourselves. This is where internal validation comes into play.

For those who are followers of Jesus, like me, think not only about your own voice in your head, but the voice of God who promises to never fail you nor forsake you (Hebrews 13:5). God made you from love to be loved, meaning you are so extremely valuable. By sharing that with you in His word, God is validating you as worthy of love, time, and attention. I would explain this type of validation as internal, because if you are a believer of God, then you have the Holy Spirit living inside you (1 Corinthians 6:19). The Holy Spirit affirms (AKA validates) your worth and guides you in discipline, self-denial, and good character development.

And whether you are a Jesus follower or not, the currency of confidence can still bring validation into your life. Here's how.

Any of the tools that create a currency of confidence in your life where you serve and sacrifice for others will give you internal validation. Why? When you do them, you prove to yourself consistently that your actions support the confidence you feel. This means you can decide, based on your disciplined actions, that you *are* worthy of love. Validation is such a strong force in the life of every human, but internal validation is more powerful than external validation—especially as you grow in age and life experience.

This goes back to the boat example. If you felt pressured to buy a boat because you want to feel as valuable as your neighbor, that is external validation. The boat doesn't prove you are worthy of love or that you are valuable. And lying to your spouse about that kind of purchase is giving into the negative force that wants to keep you average. With internal validation—the kind that is built up over time as you multiply your currency of confidence—you can become a leader that inspires others to believe in themselves too (with or without the boat).

This is why internal validation helps us show up as the leaders that people at home and at work really need.

Feeling disciplined, confident, and validated gives you the inner strength to say, "Yes! I can do this!" And as a leader, you can pass that same confidence to the people in your life by giving them the tools to increase their currency of confidence as well.

Yet another way to set yourself up to become the kind of servant leader that can change the world is to set the correct expectations for yourself and others, which is what we're going to look at in chapter 13.

Summary

- Training in discomfort leads to discipline, and having discipline will build your confidence.
- Self-denial practices are a gift we can give ourselves to further develop our discipline.
- Taking disciplined actions helps you build confidence because you are having small victories with consistency.
- When we have the discipline to avoid temptation, we can improve our character, which makes us better leaders.
- Spiritual and physical development through discipline are both important.
- Internal validation will help you show up as the leader your team and family need.

Actions to Take

Choose a Self-Denial Practice

Now that you've read about how beneficial self-denial is and how it builds discipline, confidence, and validation, I want to encourage you to choose a self-denial practice for yourself. Here are the things you need to note when designing your routine to create more discipline in your life.

Answer the following questions to create your own self-denial practice:

1. What practice can I do daily that will help me build discipline?
2. Is this something I already like, or am I really pushing myself to engage in self-denial?
3. When am I going to start this practice and how often am I going to do it?
4. When am I going to stop this practice?
5. Whom am I going to tell about this practice so that they can keep me accountable?

If you are having a hard time thinking about which self-denial practice might work for you, a few to consider are fasting from food, skipping certain things you love (like beer and watching fútbol matches), or engaging in activities you don't like but that are good for you (like certain types of exercise or services you can do for others).

I want to remind you here that self-denial is only one tool you can use to create currency in confidence. Feel free to exercise using the different tools in this chapter as you work to build more confidence for yourself. Self-denial is a place to start.

Chapter 13

SETTING EXPECTATIONS

You have to set realistic expectations ahead of time—even if
that means you acknowledge discomfort is on the way.
—A Dr. Dan One-Liner

A s we move into this chapter, we're going to build on the ideas of development and confidence by embracing something that can feel difficult for leaders: setting appropriate expectations.

When you have confidence in yourself, your word, and the people around you, that's when you can sit in the discomfort that comes along with being honest—even about difficult circumstances or outcomes.

When I was in dental school, my professors would say over and over again, "You have to set realistic expectations with your patients." They would go on to use this example: "When referring to a denture case, tell them 'This prosthesis looks like teeth, but it is not made of real teeth. It's a piece of plastic that will sit on your gums. And it will be uncomfortable for some time.'" Our professors went on to explain that if we set the patients' expectations for something ahead of time, then when our patients were finished working with us, they would understand the entire process involved, including the adjustment period for the new prosthesis. That way, they wouldn't expect that what we had put in their mouth would function the way their actual teeth did—because it wasn't actually teeth. The denture is something artificial.

Honestly, this lesson wasn't something I remembered when I was going through my first clinical practices with patients. When we don't set expectations well, this affects the way other people interact with us and the results we've promised to get for them. In dentistry, this looks like a disappointed and discouraged patient. At home, this looks like setting unrealistic expectations for our family about what can happen when chaos enters the picture.

As it turned out, I got to see the results of not setting expectations for a patient firsthand. Allow me to explain.

My very first denture patient was my uncle. First, we had to do extractions of the teeth he had left so that he could wear a denture. But it went beyond simply taking the teeth out so he could pop the denture right in. He had to wait for the extractions to heal. When you get an extraction, it takes three months for a patient to heal before we can do a permanent set of dentures. During this healing period, we typically use what we call a temporary denture. In this case, he opted out of having a temporary denture, so he could only eat soft foods for three months.

I'm sure you can imagine that part wasn't fun. Well-made soup is delicious, but my uncle expressed that he wanted something he could sink his teeth into (pun intended). He wanted real food.

While he was healing up, I went to work creating his denture. I was focused on the tasks I needed to complete, which meant I was not so focused on communicating with my uncle about what the outcome would be. I hadn't explained the whole process, and I hadn't set the proper expectations. Timewise, in dental school, everything you do has to be approved by professors, so the process takes way longer. This meant that my uncle had to wait twice as long to even get his denture. His mouth had been healed for a while when I finally got everything for his denture approved. I'm sure you can imagine why my uncle was feeling pretty anxious to finally get his new denture and to be able to use it.

Finally, the day came for him to get his prosthesis; his denture was complete. The timing was perfect, in my uncle's opinion. He was getting it on my grandmother's birthday, which meant amazing food—steak. And he had definitely gotten tired of his mostly soup diet.

When the birthday dinner arrived, I watched as my uncle struggled intensely with his denture. I kept thinking, *Oh no, I did something wrong*. Eventually, he got up and left the table. When he came back, I realized he had taken his denture out so that he could actually eat something, even if it wasn't the steak he was previously promised.

When I talked to my professors about what had gone wrong, they told me that I hadn't set the right expectations for my uncle, and that I hadn't set correct expectations for myself as my uncle's dentist.

You see, I hadn't told my uncle early on that his denture was a plastic prosthesis and explained what that meant for his eating and food choices.

It's similar to when someone gets an artificial leg. They don't expect to run a marathon that first day. And that is exactly what my uncle had attempted by trying to eat steak on day one of using his denture—he attempted to run a marathon of the mouth.

Before he even had the procedure, I should have set his expectations by telling him he wasn't going to be able to eat steak on the first night of getting his denture. In fact for the first week, he would need a soft diet, one that required less chewing. And then over the next three weeks, he could work his way up to food that was tougher to chew. Realistically, it would probably take a month of using the denture to get used to it, and that meant it would be a whole extra month before he could eat a decent meal.

And as a dentist, I should have reminded myself what I learned in school, which was that the true efficiency of a denture is usually around 15% based on how well the patient can chew, their comfort level, and their ability to keep the denture in place while it is being used. That means the inefficiency of such a prosthesis—on average—is 85%!

The importance of setting expectations is true in life, not just dentistry. And especially for leaders, it is our job to set the expectations for the people we lead, which I'll explain in the next section.

Expect the Worst, *Don't* Hope for the Best

In chapter 11, we talked about how leaders must learn to expect chaos. And this isn't just something that we have to do for ourselves. In the last section, you can see that I didn't set my uncle up to expect the chaos that happens when you get a new prosthesis. It was my job as his doctor to lead him and set him up to succeed. Instead, he felt like he did something wrong when he couldn't use the denture right away.

As we've discussed, we need to help the people we lead, both at work and at home, to understand that chaos is unavoidable. This is especially true during transitions. And the way we help others realize and work through transitions—so that they can also train in discomfort—is by setting realistic expectations for them so they can, then, set realistic expectations for others.

When it comes to setting expectations, I often hear people say, "Expect the worst, hope for the best." But I don't agree with that line of thinking. What I often say is, "Expect the worst, *don't* hope for the best," and there are two big reasons for this.

First, I don't want people to think of hope as meaning that we're wishing for something to happen. I believe that hope is tied directly to someone's faith in God. When we hope, we are trusting that when God says He will work out everything, even the difficult things, for the best in our lives (which we see in

Romans 8:28), that He means it. When we think about what "best" means, it might mean something different to us than it does to God since He is all knowing (omniscient) and is able to see the entire picture of our lives—something we can't see.

I believe chaos is inevitable, and if my team or family only hopes for amazing and happy things, they won't be ready for hard moments. Wishing for only the best things to happen every day—from our limited perspectives of only being able to see the past and the moment we are in right now—won't set up the people we lead to navigate chaos well. It all begins with setting the right expectations for them and helping them to do the same for others.

To help us understand how this works, we're going to look at a few practical examples of what setting expectations well can look like.

This Is Going to Hurt

One of the earlier examples I used in the book was that if we tell a dental patient that the procedure they are having isn't going to be a big deal—and then they experience pain—they are going to feel upset.

Why?

Because we haven't left room for what could really happen to them: We haven't set a realistic expectation.

If we tell the patient they are going to experience some pain (which is definitely a possibility), and then they don't, they feel great! But if we don't tell them about the potential complications and pain that can result from whatever procedure they're having—if we don't set expectations of the chaos that can enter the scenario—we aren't setting *proper* expectations.

For example, a worst case scenario for a robust procedure could be an infection requiring antibiotics. So what happens when we explain what *could* go wrong and everything ends up being fine and chaos-free? They avoided the most difficult outcome, which we placed in their minds so that they would know what to expect, and they are thankful they didn't have to deal with the worst case scenario.

There is an important distinction to make here. Setting correct expectations is *not* the same as discouraging people. When we tell a dental patient that they will experience some pain, it isn't to discourage them from going through with the procedure. It is to help them understand how a measured amount of chaos can come into their lives as a result of a procedure—so that they know how to prepare for what is coming.

The goal of discouragement is to prevent someone from doing something. Setting an expectation helps them realistically prepare for what's coming. That's the difference. In general, setting proper expectations is a way to *encourage* others that they can manage whatever chaos comes their way.

Now that you know what this looks like in a dental office, let's see what this looks like at home.

When I was seeking to avoid serving my family at home (which I explained in chapter 11 as being caused by the pride I hadn't battled against), I wasn't setting the right expectations for myself as a father. That meant I was also failing to set the proper expectations for my wife and kids.

At that time, I basically wanted to teach them to expect me to prioritize my comfort *over* them. That was an impossible expectation for all of us, and it caused a lot of frustration, as you know—for me and for my family. The reason mine was an impossible expectation is because chaos *will* come and disrupt comfort. That is the reality of how life works.

Recently, my family took a trip to Rome, Italy, but it wasn't the kind of typical vacation we had done before. This time, our trip was focused primarily on historic sites (and some gelato, because when in Rome). One of my sons has autism, and one beauty of having a child with autism is that they are extremely honest. So, I kept thinking, *What if he tells me he hates going to all of these historic sites, what am I going to do? How will I deal with this?* Based on the way my son communicates, I needed to prepare myself, or set the expectation for myself, to be ready to adjust my own plans so I could address his feelings. And I became willing, ahead of time, to sacrifice some of my time going through those sites to make sure that my son was enjoying the trip too.

But my son absolutely loved everything! That made the trip even more amazing for me. I had prepared for chaos to come into our trip, but then it didn't. This is how setting expectations works.

There were definitely still moments of chaos on our vacation, because that's what happens when you travel. But I had expected them, and that allowed me to recognize the beauty of the time we had together as a family, even when things weren't going according to plan.

This emphasizes why I don't believe we should plan for the worst and hope for the best. Yes, we should plan for chaos and set the correct expectations, but we don't know what best really is through our limited perspectives. And when we train for chaos and expect it, and then chaos takes a break, we find that the resulting moments are so much sweeter (just like Italian gelato).

This is the same joy a dental patient feels when you tell them that they *will* experience pain, and then it turns out to be mild.

There are moments, though, when chaos seems to be winning, and that can feel hard when this turns out to be a long-term experience. But we can still have faith that God has a plan in the midst of chaos. That's what Jesus taught us: He set the expectations for His followers when He said, "If the world hates you, know that it has hated me before it hated you" (John 15:18).

By using the example of the hatred Jesus faced in His own life, he set the expectation that some people would be angry to hear that He was sent into the world to save it as the Son of God. So as His followers who share his hope-filled message, we can expect to meet that same resistance. He knew when we shared about Him, it wasn't going to be easy, so He set the expectation in John 15 for what we would face. That's what effective leadership looks like.

So what do we do, then, when chaos is a long-term visitor?

When Chaos Seems to Be Taking Over

I am friends with an amazing priest who was assigned to a parish that had a school. Over time, that school gained a reputation of being elite, attracting many families who prioritized academic excellence over a faith-based education.

The priest felt that it was his responsibility to refocus the school on what had been the main idea when it was founded, and he told the staff, students, and parents, "We have to go back to our roots and focus our attention on faith. That is why this school exists, and we need to honor that."

Many of the parents who were seeking academic excellence over faith were extremely upset about this shift. They hadn't chosen the school for their kids because it was a Catholic school, and they didn't want it to feel like a Catholic school. They were frustrated that the school would try to incorporate more of an emphasis on faith to get back to the school's vision and mission. So what did these parents do?

They went to the media to complain that the priest was "forcing" the students to go to Adoration and Mass. But that wasn't true at all. What actually happened was that the priest encouraged the students to go back to Adoration and Mass, and a lot of them did. However, the students who weren't as interested in the faith aspect of the school said they felt peer pressure to go even though they didn't want to. To be clear, there was only encouragement for them to attend the Mass, but no forcing of behavior.

As a result, many families left the school. And my friend, the priest, was discouraged. I hated to see him like that, but I knew I needed to help him realize which expectations he should set for what I anticipated would be a long-term experience with chaos.

Although I knew the priest could already guess what I was going to say, I wanted to encourage him. I reminded him, "Father, don't forget: This rejection is a sign that you are doing the good work of God, and Jesus told us in John 15:18 that if people hated Him, they will hate us too. This means that the rejection is actually a good sign, and we don't know yet exactly what God is going to do through this. Only He knows."

Today, the school is flourishing! It was difficult for a few years as the school shifted its focus of attention back to faith, and there were even times when it looked like the school would have to close. But it didn't.

As it turned out, that season of long-term chaos is exactly what God used to refocus the school on its mission. Even though the negative press and the upset parents were a struggle for my friend to confront, over time, the pressure of working through these issues united the remaining students and parents to the mission the school should have been prioritizing all along. And the end result was something that the students, staff, and parents could be thankful for: a place to educate kids that prioritized building up their faith. The result of this long-term chaos was gratitude on the part of everyone who stayed and believed in the mission.

When we go through something like this—prolonged seasons of chaos—the last thing we want to feel is gratitude. I understand that, really. But the truth is that when chaos has decided to stay as a long-term guest, we can still have faith that there is something beautiful that will come of it. I have seen this time and time again in my own life and the lives of the people I am blessed enough to lead.

So, if you are experiencing something difficult that lasts weeks, months, or years, try your best to look at what you can still be grateful for in the midst of that situation to encourage yourself. You have prepared for chaos. You have trained in discomfort. And that means that when anything comes into your life that feels hard, you can still encourage yourself that something good will come, even if the end results aren't what you were hoping for or don't happen within your idea of good timing.

Back in chapter 12 we talked about how we can build currency by training in chaos. This idea is one we're building on here, because confidence affects our ability to set realistic expectations. How? When we can trust ourselves to face chaos, we can also communicate potential chaos to ourselves and the people around us, as we feel prepared to deal with it. I want you to know, wonderful reader, that if you can learn to build currency in confidence and to train in discomfort, then you will be able to set expectations well, not only for yourself but for everyone around you.

And if you can lead the people in your life in a way that helps *them* set the right expectations for themselves and the people around them, you will inspire people to change the world for the better. They will know how to navigate chaos whether it is in the short-term or it stays awhile.

As we close out this chapter, get ready to take a journey into your past where you can practice facing a prolonged moment of chaos to help you understand what you would do differently now that you're armed with the knowledge in this book.

Then, we'll discuss how the power trio of faith, courage, and enthusiasm can transform your leadership forever.

Summary

- When we set expectations well, we will avoid being let down or frustrated in the future.
- Not managing expectations can cause confusion and make relationships feel more difficult.
- Leaders need to get people ready for chaos by letting them know that every person will experience feeling uncomfortable in every environment at some point.
- Setting proper expectations gives people the strength to deal with hardship instead of working to avoid it (which is impossible).
- Being ready for chaos makes you stronger; hoping for what you think is best won't help you accomplish what you need to do.
- Hope comes from having faith, not just wishing that certain things would happen.
- Expecting the worst makes you value the times when things go well in a more intense way.
- In life, long-term chaos can sharpen our senses of purpose and bring us closer to our visions and missions.

Actions to Take

In the exercise for this chapter, let's practice setting better expectations by changing the way you look at a negative experience you've been through—during a time when chaos was a long-term resident in your life.

Grab your journal or phone (something to write in) and go through the following prompts as you learn how you could have set expectations differently in the past to engage long-term chaos in a more prepared way.

1. Write down a time when you felt caught off guard, frustrated, or disappointed by something that happened. Then write down answers to the questions below:
   » What were you expecting to happen when that specific brand of chaos became a long-term presence in your life?
   » As you look back, think about whether those expectations were based on what you *thought* could happen or what you *wanted* to happen. Which expectations did you have?
2. Were there signs that showed you chaos might be coming that you felt tempted to ignore? What were they?
   » If you had acknowledged those signs, could you have prepared better?
   » Would others around you have been able to prepare better?
3. Think about what you would do now if you were to go back and revisit that moment—how would you set expectations differently?
   » What would you tell yourself or the others around you to help prepare for the discomfort that ultimately came?

» How would you encourage yourself to deal with delays or setbacks in that case today (based on what you read in this chapter)?

4. Did you feel gratitude for the potential of what could come from that season? If not, how would you encourage yourself today to cultivate gratitude if you were in that same long-term season of chaos now?

» Were you wishing for things to be different, or were you hoping that even in that extended time of chaos, something better than what you had started with would come from that experience?

5. What unexpected insight, growth, or strength (which are all gifts) came out of your long-term experience with chaos?

» How would have you been able to better recognize those new gifts if you had set better expectations sooner in that experience?

Amazing work. By doing this exercise and learning what you could have done differently in a chaotic situation, you have mentally prepared for your next encounter with chaos. And I trust you will set expectations well when you and chaos meet again.

Chapter 14

FAITH, COURAGE, AND ENTHUSIASM—TOOLS TO TRANSFORM YOUR LIFE

I can learn.
—A Dr. Dan One-Liner (This is inspired by an
extremely special person.)

As we bring our time together in these pages to a close, there is one more thing on my heart to teach you: I want to show you the power of faith, courage, and enthusiasm combined.

When you take everything we've covered so far in this book and combine those principles with what I am going to teach you in this chapter, you will become a leader who is an unstoppable force for good. Now, you don't have to get every single thing right to see that happen. I certainly haven't (as you've seen in my story). But you do have to be willing to learn.

There are still so many things I *don't* know. We've already talked about how as professional leaders, part of our responsibility is to be able to recognize and hire people who have amazing skills and unique talents to do the things we don't know how to do well—or do at all. But there is another skill that is vital to every leader: the ability to learn.

With that critical skill in mind, this is when the power trio of faith, courage, and enthusiasm comes in. After that, there is one final story I want to share—one that perfectly captures everything I know about believing "I have the ability to learn." It's a story that is dear to my heart, that I've been saving for this final chapter, and it's about one of the most influential people in my life (a beautiful soul I haven't introduced to you yet). My grandmother.

We begin with faith, courage, and enthusiasm.

The Power Trio

Before you learn how this power trio works together, we have to define the individual concepts first. Let's take a look.

Faith

What does the word faith mean?

Faith is an active trust that we place in the people and things around us. It isn't just a thought we have—faith is what moves us to take action. Think of faith as an invisible bridge that appears when you step onto it. Before you put your foot out, you don't know if anything is there. But as you step forward, suddenly you find your foot lands on solid ground. That is how faith behaves in our lives.

We cannot see what will happen in the future, but we still take that step forward, having faith that as we walk out into the universe—each and every day—we will be able to accomplish our individual missions.

The concept of faith is one we've touched on throughout this book. But here, I want to break down the different ways that I believe faith shows up in our daily lives, whether that's at home or at work.

The four aspects (or categories) of faith are:

- Faith in God
- Faith in Myself
- Faith in Others
- Faith in My Goals (Leading to Faith in My Mission)

Let's talk about faith in God first. Dear reader, you already know how passionate I am about my faith in God. Without that relationship, I wouldn't be the leader I've become today. It is my faith in God that gives me the strength to act, because I believe He has a mission for me: one that I want to accomplish not only for myself, but for His people and His Kingdom.

As a reminder, here is my personal mission, which I shared in chapter 2:

It is my hope to inspire each and every one of my team members to embrace the power and value they have to transform someone else's life using their unique talents.

We also spoke about how God has loved each one of us into existence; we were all created by love. And that is why I believe the most important faith to start with is faith in God's love for us. He is the one who has made possible all the things that have happened in my life and in the lives of the friends, family members, and saints, those who I have shared about in this book.

Even if you don't believe in God, you can acknowledge that the circumstances and resources that have come into your life have helped you succeed by providing you with opportunities. You can see that the resources related to these opportunities have also taught you important things and given you wonderful moments in your life.

While I acknowledge that everyone has the potential to experience amazing circumstances whether they believe in God or not, I will say that I believe that the love and acceptance we find from others in the world comes from God Himself. I have experienced that personally so many times through the years, and that is one of the reasons I was so motivated to write this book for leaders everywhere.

Next, let's talk about what "faith in myself" means.

In chapter 12, we talked about the currency of confidence. Using the tools I mentioned in that chapter, we have the ability to continually create confidence currency. As we do, we create an understanding of who we are and the good we can do. This directly shapes how much faith we can have in ourselves.

Earlier in the book, I also mentioned that I believe false humility has a different definition than the one that is most often used. I would say that false humility happens when I think that my value is lower than anyone else's. Realizing and believing in my value and avoiding giving into false humility are also part of having faith in myself.

Having faith in myself means that I can trust myself to take the action I need to take to complete my mission.

And when I've proven to myself that I can show up consistently and use my gifts and talents while acknowledging my own value, that is when I can trust myself not only to take action—but to lead others to take action as well. That brings us into the next aspect of faith: faith in others.

Having faith in others, this means we trust *them* to take action. And as leaders, this means we take this trust one step further and allow others to act on our behalf: They are representing us directly with their actions. This is vital to leaders because we can not act alone, which takes us to our last aspect of faith: faith in our goals.

Finally, there is faith in goals. This means we trust that our goals are worthy of our time and effort. And as we take action to accomplish these goals, step by step, we are also trusting that our goals will bring us to a place where we're able to live out each of our individual missions.

When you combine these four types of faith (in God, yourself, others, and your goals), you will be able to lead from a position of trust. You know in your heart that you can step out onto that invisible bridge and four different forces will be holding you.

That leads into our next part of the power trio. When your faith is strong, you can use it to take courageous action.

Courage

I cannot tell you how many times I've heard people call me a "fearless leader" over the last decade. But it's not true. Here's why. I laugh when I hear someone say this because *of course,* I experience fear like any other leader does. *Of course,* I feel afraid sometimes. That's part of being a human.

The great thing about being courageous is that it means you can still *take action* even when you are *afraid*.

When you have courage, you can attempt to do difficult things. And when you stack courage on top of faith, you are at a place where you can be an unstoppable leader. This is where the idea, "I have the ability to learn," really takes flight (as you are about to see in the final story I share). At that point, you only need one more thing: enthusiasm, the third component in the power trio.

Enthusiasm

In chapter 13, I mentioned that to me, hope is so much more than wishful thinking. Hope is a specific brand of trust that lives in me even when everything feels like it's going wrong. In these situations, hope tells me that I can trust God with the long-term vision He has for my life. He sees all of the puzzle pieces of my time on Earth, and only He knows how they fit together. He can see the big picture right now, and I can't.

Enthusiasm comes into play when I apply joy to the hope I have that the big picture of what is happening in my life will help me accomplish my goals. That is why enthusiasm is the mechanism that brings me into alignment with my mission.

The word *enthusiasm* comes from the Greek word *entheos*, which means "in God." That is why I use this word specifically as the final concept in the power trio: It beautifully illustrates the kind of deep fire of joy that is lit by faith for a person or an opportunity. Enthusiasm is courage *with* joy, and when we add that joyful courage to our faith—that is when we can approach everyone we lead in a way that inspires them to come alongside us as we work to live out our goals and missions.

When it comes to how we lead, enthusiasm can create a bridge that carries the faith of our hearts to others so that we can awaken their courage too. Then they are also able to cross that invisible bridge, and they are excited to do so! Why? Enthusiasm is contagious.

When you combine faith, courage, and enthusiasm, that is when you pass the torch of hope, purpose, and transformation to the people you lead at home or at work.

Amazing reader, the story I want to close out the book with illustrates all three of these concepts and how they work together as a power trio. Let's take a look at how my grandmother was able to use all three components to create the life she needed—in the wake of the tragedy that happened when my grandfather passed away and my grandmother became a single mom.

If Abuela Can Learn, So Can I

My father is from a large family, and he was the youngest of seven children, which means that when I was growing up, I had an older *abuela* (grandmother). Most of what I remember her doing was resting.

Even though she didn't have the energy to chase me around or play with me, visiting her was still always a bright shining moment in my life. I was so excited whenever I got a chance to be with her.

When I was a young boy, my abuela lived with my aunt, and when we would have family gatherings, I would always go straight to my abuela's room. At first, that was because she always had a treat ready to share with me. And while the treats were my primary motivation when I was a small boy, what kept me going back to that room was my abuela's stories. And there was one story in particular that would go on to shape my life in an intense way.

Me as a young boy with my loving abuelita, Chela

My abuela didn't have an easy life. As I mentioned, she had 7 children (including my father), and when she was 38 years old, my *abuelo* (grandfather) died, making my abuela a widow with 7 kids to take care of.

My dad was only three years old when my abuelo died, and that meant my abuela had to learn to do all sorts of things she wasn't used to. She had to be the mom and the dad. She had to be the homemaker and the breadwinner.

The thing about my abuela that really stuck with me was her faith. She was a woman of great faith (which we'll see in detail in just a little bit). Someone might look at a family with 7 kids and question, "To have the husband and father die when he was 39 years old, leaving his wife and children behind, how can God be good if He allowed something like that to happen?"

But my grandmother *never* thought like that. In no way did she reject God when her husband died. She saw what was happening as an opportunity to trust God even more—she said she didn't have any other choice because there weren't any other options. She *had* to trust God. She would say, "God has the full picture. He can see beyond what I can see."

Her faith and belief didn't mean her situation was easy. She knew that she needed to get a job to provide for her family. Her challenge was that she didn't know how to do anything outside of the home. When my abuelo was around, my abuela stayed with the kids while he went out and worked.

One day my abuela saw a job opening for someone to sew shirts. The next thing she did was purely motivated by courage. Though my abuela had never done anything to do with sewing in her life up until that point, when the company manager asked what experience she had, she replied confidently, as the true leader of her family, "I can learn."

My abuelita, Chela, was a determined person

However, the sewing job didn't pay enough to cover all of her expenses as the breadwinner of her family. She knew she needed to find something else. So she applied for another job she wasn't qualified for—the Executive Assistant for the Department of Education in Peru. It was a government job, which meant good benefits for her children. But she had only ever done factory work. As she prayed about what to do, she believed God wanted her to act in faith and to try for the job, even though she didn't have the qualifications she needed.

On the day of the interview, my abuela said her prayers, got dressed in her nicest clothes, and went down to the government office. When she was in the elevator, a man walked in; he didn't push any button because he was headed to the same floor as my abuela. She stood there waiting for the elevator to ascend, and the man started to talk to her. He asked what she was doing there, and she told him that she was there to apply for a job.

Once they arrived at the floor where they both got off, the man walked into the office with my abuela where her interview would be. He told her good luck and left.

Next, my abuela focused on the first round of interviews. They asked her, "Have you ever done this before?" She told them, "No, but I can learn." After a short conversation, the person asked my abuela to go into another office, where she had a second interview. In her third, and final interview, the person sitting behind the desk said, "Well, this is the last interview." They looked down at a paper on their desk that had notes written about my abuela and said, "I see here that you are recommended by the Secretary of Education."

My abuela had no idea what this person was talking about. Finally, he looked at her and said, "He is the one who walked you into the interview."

The Secretary of Education had never met my abuela before that day, but because he stayed to talk to her for a little after their elevator ride, the entire interviewing staff took that as him recommending her for the job. In Spanish, my abuela told me later that this was a coincidence given by God, which in English we might call a God wink.

Every time my abuela reached this point in the story, she would burst into laughter. To this day, I miss her laugh very much. Then she would say, "Suddenly, they gave me the job!"

She was the most unqualified person for that executive assistant position, but she did learn what she needed to do and spent the rest of her career there.

By sharing this story, my abuela was leading me to learn what I needed to know. That I could have faith in God's plan for my life like she did. That if I didn't know something, I could learn to adjust (which I talk more about in my second book). And I never forgot her approach of "I can learn."

When it came time for me to find my way in the United States as an immigrant dentist from Peru without a license to practice dentistry, I needed that same attitude of "I can learn." I didn't go back to dental school so I could get licensed in the United States. You saw in my story how hard it was for me to make it through dental school the first time because it was expensive. What I didn't know was that God would open up another way for me to get into the dental business in the United States.

You see, I had the opportunity to become a business investor in one of five states that allowed someone who was unlicensed to be the owner of a dental practice. But I had to become a business professional to make this happen. I didn't have an MBA or any formal business education, and I certainly didn't have the experience I needed. But I thought, *I can learn.* Thankfully, my abuela's method worked and I was able to learn what I needed to know.

The rest of that story is for another book (coming soon). I hope you can see that my abuela's attitude and wisdom taught me how to be in a world where I wasn't the most qualified person. I was able to remember my abuela's leaps of faith, and that inspired me to take many leaps of my own.

That is what inspiring leaders do: They take leaps of faith, like my abuela.

How to Take Leaps as a Leader

As I've walked my path of leadership, everything started with a sense of trust in God. That trust moved me to understand I was unique and therefore had unique value. The same is true for you.

You are talented, and you have a mission that no one else can do. You were loved into this life, and you have an opportunity to value and honor the sacrifices of everyone who helped you become you by living your mission.

If you don't believe in God, you still can believe in the people who have shaped your life: the people who raised you, your teachers, and everyone who showed you that they *believed in you* all along the way.

The best way to honor the sacrifices that others have made for you and the ones that you have made for yourself is to keep going in life. Use faith, courage, and enthusiasm to become a leader who inspires others in the world to be better—one person at a time.

My abuela worked and sacrificed in order to honor her husband by putting the love he had shown to his family during his lifetime into all of the things she did. On her journey, she had to do many uncomfortable things, and it is my abuela who set an amazing example for me of what training in discomfort looked like. Yes, she had to do things she preferred not to do, but she had faith, and to that she added courage, and to that courage she added enthusiasm. The power trio!

One thing my abuela always said was that she was blessed with the task of raising my father and his siblings without a husband. This wasn't her plan, but she embraced the way she could impact the lives of her children and her mission of passing on the love my abuelo had for his family even after he was gone. She was a leader to the entire family, including me!

And you are blessed with the gift of leadership. Not everyone is blessed with this gift, so please don't take this position of influence for granted. It's a big responsibility, but it will lead to big gifts in different areas of your life. When you are a sacrificial leader, like my abuela was, and when you deny yourself for the sake of others, your choices will make you a better mother, father, wife, husband, son, or daughter. Why? Because that is love in action. And putting love into action will also make you a better team leader.

When I'm speaking at a conference to other leaders, I often end with something like this:

As a leader, don't limit yourself or your impact out of a fear of failure. You have the courage to transform any environment you enter.

With that statement in mind, take a moment to think back to chapter 2. There, you learned how to understand your mission so that you could live out your vision. As I close these pages and our journey together, I want to remind you that as long as you are convinced of your mission and your vision, you will find a way to make it happen.

Now, go out and lead. You have everything you need (and more) to become an inspiring leader that changes the world through love—one person at a time.

BEFORE WE SAY GOODBYE

As one last gift to you, I have created a comprehensive assessment in the appendix that is based on everything you've learned as we went through this book together. Please feel free to take it now and each month moving forward as you look for specific marks of your leadership to improve. It will help you determine what your next focus of discipline should be as you work to become yet another leader that humanity needs.

And as a final encouragement, I would love to speak this over your life, wonderful reader:

> The LORD bless you and keep you:
> The LORD make his face to shine upon you, and be gracious to you:
> The LORD lift up his countenance upon you, and give you peace.
>
> –Numbers 6:24-26

With all the love in my heart,

Dr. Dan

Appendix

THE COMPREHENSIVE
LEADERSHIP ASSESSMENT

As we close out the book together, I want to help you review everything we've talked about during this journey. So for your final action to take, I want to give you an assessment that will show how much you've grown and which areas to focus on as you continue that growth.

First, we're going to go through the 7 marks of leadership:

- Integrity
- Respect
- Positivity
- Empathy
- Teamwork
- Service
- Humility

After that, you'll go through assessments for the combined skills we covered in part 2 of the book:

- Training in Being Uncomfortable (Training for Chaos)

- The Currency of Confidence
- Setting Expectations

As you work your way through each section, mark which answers are true for you by circling "T" and which ones that are false for you by circling "F." Then, tally up your points for each part.

Each answer that is marked as "T" is worth one point.

If you score over three points in a specific section, you are doing great—keep going. If you score below three—refer back to the related section in the book to help you focus on improving those elements first, before you focus on overall growth.

You are unique and created by love to be a leader that will change the world—one person at a time. You've got this.

Your Vision and Mission

I believe that every person, including myself, was created with value and purpose.

Circle one: T or F

I can clearly explain my personal and professional missions and how they guide my leadership.

Circle one: T or F

I rely on my long-term vision to stay motivated and to help others stay focused during challenges.

Circle one: T or F

I consider myself a visionary leader who helps others get excited about a shared mission.

Circle one: T or F

I believe that greatness comes from consistent small actions aligned with a meaningful mission—not only big accomplishments.

Circle one: T or F

How many did you mark T for True? __

How many did you mark F for False? __

Holiness, Integrity, Trust, and Relationship

I intentionally spend quiet time in reflection or meditation to align my actions with my values.

Circle one: T or F

I would not compromise my integrity by taking shortcuts or making decisions that don't reflect my highest standards.

Circle one: T or F

I believe that living with integrity in both personal and professional settings builds trust and long-term influence.

Circle one: T or F

When I feel overwhelmed, I pause to reflect, refocus, and reconnect with my core purpose before I continue forward.

Circle one: T or F

I see leadership as a responsibility to invest in my own growth and in developing the unique strengths of others.

Circle one: T or F

How many did you mark T for True? __

How many did you mark F for False? __

Respecting the Innate Value of Others

I believe every person has unique value and deserves to be treated with admiration and care.

Circle one: T or F

I often take time to understand others before forming opinions, knowing that respect begins with truly seeing someone.

Circle one: T or F

I don't struggle to show respect to others because I have learned to respect and care for myself.

Circle one: T or F

I try to imagine what others might be going through so I can respond with compassion, even when I'm upset or hurt.

Circle one: T or F

I see respect as something that can be modeled and passed on, and I try to lead by example in how I treat others.

Circle one: T or F

How many did you mark T for True? __

How many did you mark F for False? __

Thoughts of Positivity and Feelings of Joy

I believe that small positive actions can inspire others and create a ripple effect of encouragement.

Circle one: T or F

I often focus more on what's going right than on the bad things happening around me.

Circle one: T or F

I make a conscious effort to encourage others, especially when they're doing things well.

Circle one: T or F

I tend to judge others on their full potential instead of judging them quickly based on their mistakes.

Circle one: T or F

I try to avoid gossip and instead choose to speak in ways that uplift others and build a positive future with them.

Circle one: T or F

How many did you mark T for True? __

How many did you mark F for False? __

Engaging Empathy and Embracing Mercy

I make an effort to understand how others want to be treated, rather than assuming they see the world the way I do.

Circle one: T or F

I feel that even when I'm busy or overwhelmed, it's important to slow down and offer genuine empathy to someone in need.

Circle one: T or F

I believe that real fulfillment comes from giving love and support without expecting anything in return.

Circle one: T or F

I recognize that people are shaped by their experiences, and I try to respond with understanding instead of judgment.

Circle one: T or F

When I see someone struggling, I take compassionate action rather than just feeling sympathy for them.

Circle one: T or F

How many did you mark T for True? __

How many did you mark F for False? __

The Harmony Teamwork Creates

I understand the power of expressing belief in someone, and I use it to encourage growth in others.

Circle one: T or F

I view mistakes as opportunities to collaborate with people, rather than focusing solely on problems.

Circle one: T or F

I do not avoid addressing team behavior that goes against our values, even if I worry that doing so will cause temporary conflict.

Circle one: T or F

I believe one act of belief, support, or kindness can create lasting change in someone's life.

Circle one: T or F

Even when it's time to part ways with someone on my team, I strive to do so with respect and compassion.

Circle one: T or F

How many did you mark T for True? __

How many did you mark F for False? __

Service and Sacrifices

I believe that true leadership is about serving others with humility, not leading from a place of entitlement.

Circle one: T or F

I actively model service and selflessness in my home or organization, knowing that this can influence the culture around me.

Circle one: T or F

I don't measure success mostly by achievements and material rewards, because I don't believe they bring lasting fulfillment.

Circle one: T or F

I view my leadership role—both at work and at home—as an opportunity to serve with love, not just to direct or manage.

Circle one: T or F

I believe that leading through care, sacrifice, and service inspires others to do the same.

Circle one: T or F

How many did you mark T for True? __

How many did you mark F for False? __

Humility—The Most Important Mark

I try to treat everyone I encounter as equally valuable, no matter their role or status.

Circle one: T or F

I've noticed that when I lead with humility, it strengthens unity and collaboration in my relationships and teams.

Circle one: T or F

I am not interested in measuring my worth by my title or position, and I don't let my position affect how I treat others.

Circle one: T or F

Facing my own pride has helped me grow in ways that made my personal and professional relationships healthier.

Circle one: T or F

I believe no one truly succeeds alone, and humility allows me to acknowledge and appreciate the contributions of others.

Circle one: T or F

How many did you mark T for True? __

How many did you mark F for False? __

Trained in Being Uncomfortable

I believe that pursuing greatness often requires stepping out of my comfort zone.

Circle one: T or F

The stories I tell myself influence how I respond to challenges and lead others.

Circle one: T or F

I prepare myself mentally for chaos and difficult situations before they happen.

Circle one: T or F

Training myself to face discomfort helps me grow stronger as a leader.

Circle one: T or F

I see daily challenges as opportunities to grow, even when they require sacrifice or letting go of parts of myself.

Circle one: T or F

How many did you mark T for True? __

How many did you mark F for False? __

The Currency of Confidence

I believe that training myself to face discomfort helps me develop the discipline needed to lead well.

Circle one: T or F

Practicing self-denial is something I see as valuable for personal growth and leadership.

Circle one: T or F

Small consistent actions build my confidence over time through repeated success.

Circle one: T or F

Avoiding temptations or distractions strengthens my character and improves how I lead others.

Circle one: T or F

Developing both my inner mindset and physical well-being is important for me to prioritize so that I can show up fully as a leader.

Circle one: T or F

How many did you mark T for True? __

How many did you mark F for False? __

Setting Expectations

Setting clear expectations helps prevent frustration and confusion in my relationships and teams.

Circle one: T or F

I know that uncomfortable or chaotic situations will happen, so it is my responsibility to help the people I lead set realistic expectations.

Circle one: T or F

Preparing myself and others for discomfort and hardship builds strength and resilience.

Circle one: T or F

Hope is more than wishing—it comes from having a grounded faith or confidence in what is possible.

Circle one: T or F

Experiencing long-term challenges can sharpen my sense of purpose and help me stay focused on my goals.

Circle one: T or F

How many did you mark T for True? __

How many did you mark F for False? __

GET SUPPORT AS YOU BECOME THE LEADER HUMANITY NEEDS

Daniel Tataje wrote this book to support you as you embrace the gift of leadership and he would love to hear directly from you. If you found this book helpful, please reach out to him via email by sending a message to Connect @DanielTataje.com.

And if you would like to get additional support as you walk through your own leadership journey, check out **www.DanielTataje.com**, where you can find more resources for you and your professional team as you embrace your unique mission and vision.

ACKNOWLEDGEMENTS

I want to say thank you…

First and foremost to my amazing, smart, and understanding wife—Scarlett. You are a huge blessing in my life and I couldn't have done any of the things that I wrote about in this book without you.

To my inspiring and encouraging children, I love you and thank God for you—Nathan, Ethan, Danny, Mia, Matias, and Stella. You motivate me to become a better man and father each and every day.

To my parents, for all of the sacrifices you made to help me become the man I am today, both personally and professionally.

To my older sister, Eliana, and my older brother, Edgardo. For being there to support me when I was growing up and caring for me. I appreciate you both.

Mona, what can I even say to thank you? You were the one who taught me some of the most important lessons in my life. You pointed me to Jesus. You gave me a passion for leadership. Thank you for your time and unconditional love.

Luchon, look how far we've come. The things I wrote about you in this book don't even begin to cover what an amazing influence you have had, and continue to have, on me and my family. I can't imagine how different my story would have been if you hadn't taken me in (and given me so many delicious meals). Thank you.

Mr. Serra, even though you aren't around to read this anymore, I write this to honor your legacy. Thank you for choosing me to invest your time in. I can't imagine how many people's lives have been changed because of your care and sacrifice.

To my amazing team at Mercy Dental: You made all of the things in this book possible. I am honored to work alongside you as we all work toward our collective mission.

John Drake, you have been the most amazing friend. Thank you for your intense dedication and hard work. You inspire me with your belief in what we could do together.

To my wonderful assistant and niece, Kiara Richmond, thank you for partnering with me professionally at Mercy Dental and for working with me on getting this book just right. It was a joy to be able to share the writing process with you, and I appreciate every minute and every note.

To the first person I ever employed, Rajme, who is now a Regional Manager at Mercy Dental group. You are a gift.

To my writing coach, Kristin Spencer—you are a gift from God. When I started this project, it was so daunting and definitely took me out of my comfort zone. I was praying for someone who could help me bring these concepts and stories to life, and you were the answer to that prayer. I am thankful for your time and guidance.

And, finally, to God. Thank you for creating me, loving me, and being the center of my life. And for teaching me—so patiently—all of the lessons I shared in this book (and some that were just for me).

ABOUT THE AUTHOR

Daniel Tataje grew up in Lima, Peru, with the dream of someday becoming a successful dentist. But God's path for Daniel took him to a dream bigger than what he had imagined. And now he looks back at what he's been through as a training ground for what he really needed to learn—to be able to teach others how to lead with courage and empathy.

By combining his faith with his passion to help others and the never-quit attitude he learned as he worked his way through each unique opportunity along the way, Daniel has created a compelling and proven method for inspiring professional leaders and teams based on what he calls the 7 marks of leadership. Now, not only does he use the effective leadership techniques he developed in the multiple businesses that he owns, but Daniel also helps other business owners and founders create work cultures that thrive, even in the midst of chaos.

When Daniel isn't spending time with his amazing family or running his dynamic dental group or other businesses, he loves to sing and play his guitar. It is Daniel's life mission to make the world better by investing in one person at a time while inspiring others to become the leaders they were always meant to be.